The Glorious First of June 1794

In this book the naval campaign of the Glorious First of June 1794 is explored from both British and French perspectives, setting it in its wider context of the war strategy of the rival powers. The intensity of the encounter is demonstrated through the accounts of eyewitnesses; the British failure to capture the grain convoy and the effect of its arrival in France are critically examined; and the impact of the battle on public imagination is traced through plays, prints, paintings and the artefacts and memorials by which it was commemorated.

Cover illustration: Livesay of Portsmouth's engraved battle chart, 19 May–1 June 1794, from a plot supplied by James Bowen, Master of the *Queen Charlotte*. (© The National Maritime Museum, Greenwich)

EXETER MARITIME STUDIES

General Editors: Michael Duffy and David J. Starkey

THE GLORIOUS
FIRST OF JUNE 1794

A Naval Battle and its Aftermath

edited by
Michael Duffy and Roger Morriss

UNIVERSITY
of
EXETER
PRESS

First published in 2001 by
University of Exeter Press
Reed Hall, Streatham Drive
Exeter, Devon EX4 4QR
UK
www.exeterpress.co.uk

Printed digitally since 2012

British Library Cataloguing in Publication Data
A catalogue record for this book is available from the British Library

Published in association with the

ISBN 978-0-85989-689-4

Typeset in 12/13pt Garamond 3 by Kestrel Data, Exeter

Printed and bound by CPI Group (UK) Ltd, Croydon, CR0 4YY

Contents

Illustrations

The editors and publisher would like to thank Mike Rouillard of
Exeter University for redrawing the charts in Figures 3.ii, 3.iii and 5.i
and the National Maritime Museum, Greenwich, for supplying the
source material from which they were re-drawn.

The photograph of the Monument to Captain James Montagu
in Fig. 8.iii is reproduced by courtesy of the Dean and Chapter of
Westminster.

All other illustrations in this book are reproduced by courtesy of the
National Maritime Museum, Greenwich.

1

Introduction

The Battle of the Glorious First of June 1794

Michael Duffy and Roger Morriss

On the evening of Tuesday 10 June 1794 the young MP George Canning went with his friends to the opera in London.

> We had not been there above half an hour when we perceived a degree of bustle and hurry in the lower boxes—presently the Opera stopped—people stood up, some knowing, but the greater part wondering for what reason—and Boringdon came dancing into the box where I was with the news of Lord Howe's victory. I never saw a finer or more affecting spectacle than the almost electric and universal sensation that seemed to pervade every part of the House—the transport and triumph which burst forth as soon as their astonishment subsided.[1]

According to *The Times*, the orchestra struck up 'Rule, Britannia' followed by 'God save the King' in which performers and audience joined. At Covent Garden:

> 'The colours were brought on the stage, and the House, as if inspired with one sentiment, joined in those noblest of all choruses, 'Rule Britannia'—'Britons strike home'—and 'God save the King'. All next morning the bells of London 'pealed merrily' amid constant discharges of cannon, and 'every FLAG,

excepting those bearing the THIRTEEN STRIPES [of the USA], were hoisted in compliment to Lord Howe.'

Three nights of patriotic demonstrations followed in which the mob insisted on all houses illuminating their windows in celebration of the victory and broke the windows of known opponents of the war.[2]

This was how London received the news of the first great naval victory in the Great War with Revolutionary and Napoleonic France (1793–1815) that was to leave Britain supreme on the seas throughout the nineteenth century. After the closely fought contests of the previous War of American Independence, and after a year of growing frustration when war was renewed again in 1793 as the nation waited for an action between the opposing fleets, the relief and joyous celebration at the news of the battle of the Glorious First of June was a palpable demonstration of the importance of a naval victory to a maritime people. The damage inflicted on the French fleet, six ships of the line captured and another sunk, was the greatest number in any battle since 1692. French casualties—4,200 killed and wounded and 3,300 captured—amounted to about ten per cent of their available manpower in seamen.[3] At last there was an indication of the course the naval war was likely to take. The threat of invasion —which André Delaporte and Christopher Ware show below to have been the Committee of Public Safety's designated priority task for its Atlantic fleet in 1794—was removed. So also, as Ware shows, was the danger of an anti-British armed neutrality of the smaller powers of the Baltic and the United States (the one foreign embassy in London which did not celebrate Howe's victory).

Yet, curiously, the battles of 28, 29 May and 1 June were also cause for celebration by that other maritime people, the French, who, following the Revolutionary calendar, have named them the 'combats de Prairial', Prairial being the ninth month. The French fleet was at sea for one specific purpose—to assure the safe arrival of a large convoy loaded with American flour and tropical West Indian produce (sugar, coffee, cotton etc.), and that convoy reached Brest safely two days after the battered French fleet returned to port. In his contribution below, André Delaporte

2

discusses the campaign from the French perspective. He points out how the mid-twentieth century battles for survival against totally ruthless foes have led to a reassessment of the value of the preservation of convoys, and of the tactical preservation of a fleet even with the sacrifice of key units. Delaporte delves beneath the panoply of myth and propaganda which came to surround the battle in France as well as in Britain and grapples directly with the political directives and pressures to which the French commander-in-chief, Villaret-Joyeuse, was subjected. Both Norman Hampson and William Cormack have shown how, from the arrival of the political commissioners Jeanbon Saint André and Prieur of the Marne in Brest in October 1793, the ruling Committee of Public Safety made Herculean efforts to build up the French Atlantic fleet to a position in which it could effectively contest home waters with the Royal Navy.[4] That the French mobilization was successful beyond the expectations of the British Admiralty is shown by the way in May 1794 the French were in a position to put more ships of the line into the campaign than Howe's Channel Fleet. However, Delaporte shows how the French Atlantic fleet was more or less controlled and restricted in all its actions by the instructions it received from the Committee of Public Safety. He indicates that the latter in Paris, though by no means qualified to take naval decisions (and indeed against the appeals of its naval expert Saint-André at Brest[5]), was responsible for the division of the French fleet and despatch of two divisions in opposite directions from the main battlefleet. Although one of these managed to join up with the Brest fleet in time to participate in the final First of June battle, it was not until 5 May that the Committee of Public Safety finally released the six ships of the line and two rasées it had held at Cancale in preparation for an invasion of the Channel Islands—too late for that force to get back to join Villaret-Joyeuse.[6] Delaporte also reveals how the Committee placed greater value on the preservation of the Fleet, with the later object of invading Britain, than on the immediate destruction of the British Channel Fleet. He argues that, from the French point of view, the object of the campaign was not to fight the British fleet but to deter it from attacking the convoy. Villaret-Joyeuse was sent to sea for economic and political rather than naval purposes, so that the battle was hailed as enabling the government to bring food to starving France and French jubilation at the survival of the convoy was justified, even if there were long faces at the loss of seven ships of the line.

Chris Ware provides an overview from the British perspective, showing how the battle fitted into British grand strategy and he then outlines the naval manoeuvres and their consequences. He shows how both overseas expeditions to the West Indies and naval operations nearer home were essentially connected with the aim of destroying French sea power, which had so embarrassed Britain during the War of American Independence. The strategic dilemma for the British war cabinet was where best to put its military resources: into the war on the continent against terrorist France, or into a deliberate pruning of the colonies from which France drew the wealth with which she prosecuted the war. The immediate advantages of reinforcing the foothold gained at the French naval base of Toulon had to be weighed against the long-term advantages of an expedition to conquer the French West Indies and with them the commercial power and shipping that underpinned French naval power, and each had to be further measured against the need to defend British trade from attack and the British Isles against invasion. The instructions given to Lord Howe when he took his fleet to sea in May 1794 (appended to Ware's article on page 43) reflect the many duties required of the navy in the British way of warfare. His victory at the Glorious First of June and the French losses sustained in that battle gave confidence in the capacity of the British navy to contain an invasion threat, so that fears of revolution spreading across the Channel accordingly diminished and enabled a greater focus on the West Indies in 1795–96. In contrast to the frantic belated efforts of the Committee of Public Safety to restore the French navy, Ware points out that Britain was prepared for such large-scale and widespread operations by long-term investments in the British fleet dating from the administration of Lord Sandwich. British capacity to fight battles like the Glorious First of June, as well as to mount major operations overseas, was premised on a continuity of expenditure in a sustained repair and new building programme during the 1780s and 1790s.

Roger Morriss then describes the three engagements over five days between Howe and Villaret-Joyeuse which culminated in the

Glorious First of June, illustrating the nature of the fighting from British eyewitness accounts.[7] A lieutenant watching the fighting from the British frigate *Phaeton* wrote that: 'It is allowed on all sides that there never was a more hard fought action in the seas. Those who were in Lord RODNEY'S action [the battle of the Saintes in 1782], say, that the latter bears no comparison.'[8] A participant on the opposing side too, Moreau de Jonnès, reported the French sailors' opinion that the battle was 'the hardest fought and the bloodiest of any witnessed in the eighteenth century'.[9] The eyewitness accounts presented by Morriss, three of which, by Midshipman William Parker of the *Orion*, Lieutenant Rowland Bevan of the *Brunswick* and Captain the Hon. George Cranfield Berkeley of the *Marlborough*, are here published for the first time, show how closely contested these engagements were and how severely Howe's fleet suffered as well as the French. British casualties at 290 killed and 858 wounded exceeded those of every other naval battle of the 1793–1815 wars except for Trafalgar. Howe's victory might have been still more decisive had he not allowed the French to tow away four of their dismasted ships, and it says something for the impression made by Villaret-Joyeuse in this series of actions that the exhausted sixty-eight-year-old British commander allowed himself to be persuaded to call off the chase in order to protect his captures and his own dismasted ships against the possibility of a French counter-attack. Ultimately it was better and longer training in fleet discipline, seamanship, damage repair and gun-drill which saw the British through to victory, and the lieutenant of the *Phaeton* expected that the result would be psychologically decisive: 'Although the French fought desperately, I am convinced that they will not stand such close fighting as on this day.'[10]

Michael Duffy traces the British efforts to capture the elusive convoy being escorted by Admiral Vanstabel from America. In the view of the British war minister, Henry Dundas, 'All modern wars are a contention of purse', so that the ships and the rich West Indian produce returning with the convoy were probably of as much interest to the British government as the food for starving France. The Admiralty described the convoy to Howe as 'a very large and valuable Fleet of Merchant ships' whose interception was 'an object of the most urgent importance to the success of the present war'.[11] Howe assigned a separate squadron under Admiral Montagu to intercept the convoy, but his efforts reveal the difficulties of procuring good and quick intelligence across an ocean as wide as the Atlantic. He failed to find the convoy, but he happened to be off Brest when Villaret-Joyeuse's shattered fleet returned to port. His failure to attack it, and his absence when the convoy reached Brest two days later, led to him being made the scapegoat for the failure to secure a final crowning success to the campaign.

The late Lawrence Evans rather provocatively questions whether it really mattered if the convoy reached Brest since the French transportation system was so bad that it could provide little immediate material benefit. It may well be that the only real advantage derived was the boost to public morale from the fact of its arrival. Yet this could not prevent the French government led by Robespierre from falling six weeks later. Even if the flour brought by Vanstabel's convoy reached Paris, the quantity of foodstuffs involved was insufficient to feed the population for more than a few weeks. To have been effective in stabilizing the government, foodstuffs from further convoys would have had to reach the French capital. (In fact by the summer the British had their operations on the American coast in much better order and an attempt to send a second convoy of twenty-seven ships with 41,000 barrels of flour under a frigate escort from the Delaware on 13 July was broken up next day and eleven of the convoy captured.[12]) Indeed the overland communications of Brest in particular were so bad that its most effective mode of communication with the rest of France was by sea, so that, having let the convoy in, the British might have achieved their ends as effectively by not letting it out again. Yet they failed to establish a tight blockade of Brest after their victory. They did not for some weeks receive firm news of the convoy's arrival, and they were diverted by the need to escort their own convoys across the Bay of Biscay. Perhaps also they were deterred by the need to repair their own battle damages that would make any squadron that could be assembled inferior to the French fleet in Brest. It was not until September that Howe took the Channel Fleet off Brest again. In consequence most of the ships of the convoy seem to have got away to the commercial ports further down the coast in the course of June.[13] Yet even from Nantes or Bordeaux transportation was slow (Evans calculates from three weeks to two months from Nantes to Paris depending on weather conditions) and expensive, especially where goods could not travel by canal or river, so that the value of a cargo of foodstuffs destined for Paris was easily exceeded by the costs of its carriage. Evans suggests that the French government would have been far better employed in improving France's agricultural productivity and its transportation system than in sacrificing so many of its ships of the line in importing grain that could hardly affect market prices in Paris.

Ultimately, as Pieter van der Merwe observes, popular French imagery of the battle focused not on the arrival of the convoy, but on that aspect which most appealed to the French psyche: the courage and humanity of French seamen. Contemporary and later French prints depicted the battered *Vengeur du Peuple* about to sink and displayed the heroic self-sacrifice of its seamen. A legend was created which appealed to French military pride and republican patriotism and which engendered a resurgence of sales of prints in similarly beleaguered circumstances following the creation of the Third Republic out of defeat in the Franco-Prussian War in 1871. The persistence of these values continued to give the legend of the *Vengeur* life until their validity was undermined by less uplifting experiences of war in the twentieth century. Van der Merwe shows how the battle continued to be celebrated visually in paintings, prints and in the theatre. Indeed, if the number of different published prints is a measure, public interest exceeded that for any other large-scale naval engagement in either the American War of Independence or the Revolutionary War except for the Battle of the Nile. It is also significant that a more than usually accurate visual record resulted from the presence at the battle of the first British professional 'war artist', Nicholas Pocock; the survival of his sketchbooks supplies the most direct visual connection to the battle that exists and the illustrations are reproduced in the articles by Morriss and Van der Merwe below.

Van der Merwe shows how the commercial exploitation of visual representations of the battle was also put to more humanitarian use in the theatre with lasting result. On the morning after the news of Howe's victory was received, a subscription was opened at Lloyd's for the relief of widows and children of the dead which raised 1,000 guineas in two hours. Further collections were undertaken by the corporation of Trinity House and the cities of London, Edinburgh and Dublin.[14] As part of the London effort, the MP and playwright R. B. Sheridan produced a short piece entitled *The Glorious First of June* at his Drury Lane theatre on 2 July 1794, and this seems to have been the origin of the British name for a battle fought as far as 400 miles (640 km) out in the Atlantic (very unusual in the sailing era) so that it could not be named after any adjacent landmark.[15]

If in France visual representations of the battle tended to placate critics of French losses, visual imagery in Britain supplied the need to satisfy feelings for the glories of military achievement. In the emotions it evoked, the imagery helped recompense the nation for the costs of prosecuting war. As Barbara Tomlinson shows, repayment through imagery was complemented by the preservation of militaristic relics associated with the battle, flags and medals in particular. Of these perhaps the most enduringly evocative of the Glorious First of June is the banner of the boarding division of seamen seized from the captured French 74-gun ship of the line *L'America* and now at the National Maritime Museum. Sacrifices were accepted as the price of achievement, but those sacrifices were mourned and recalled in the same spirit of militaristic achievement, rendered in fine carving on tombs and memorials. This same spirit of martial achievement also runs like a thread through the commemorative wars manufactured for sale to the public: earthenware jugs, mugs and figures, medals and medallions. As items that were valued and preserved they reveal the endurance of pride in the British part in the battle. Together such relics, commemoratives and imagery served to remind and inspire successive generations.

The articles in this volume stem from a conference held at the National Maritime Museum in Greenwich to celebrate the bicentenary of the Glorious First of June. The paper by Lawrence Evans sadly was presented posthumously, while a gap revealed by discussion at the conference has been filled by an extended version of the paper that Michael Duffy presented to the Franco-British Conference of Naval Historians at Brest in 1998.[16] The object of the Museum in organizing this gathering was to place the battle in its context and review how succeeding generations have continued to preserve the memory of an event that was accorded great significance by both participating nations, to the extent that it became immersed in myth and propaganda on both sides of the Channel. At a distance in time of two hundred years, and in order to penetrate the myths and legends, it was appropriate that representatives from both Britain and France at last be brought together in order to express viewpoints about the battle that has hitherto only received occasional airings on their respective sides of the Channel. Indeed the consequent discussion revealed how little we really know about the battle, especially those aspects appreciated by the opposite nation, and the period since the conference has been used to revise the papers and provide documentary evidence to clear up some of the uncertainties. It also became apparent how different the battle was, even from others later in the same wars. Set early in the Revolutionary War, when ideas were still based on formal set-piece line battles, the Glorious First of June seemed to belong as much to the era of the War of American Independence (of which it was the most successful example for the British) as to the later Nelsonic era of annihilation. To some extent it broke through a psychological barrier as to what could be achieved in a set-piece battle and perhaps constitutes an important transitional step to what was to follow.

This volume is thus about a major naval event. However, it broadens the context of the Battle of the Glorious First of June to include its political and economic significance; it penetrates to the level of the seamen within the societies that took part; and it examines the artistic and material legacy left to generations who would look back to the battle as part of their heritage. The editors hope that it will show that military and naval events do not happen in isolation. Though the Battle of the Glorious First of June took place in mid-Atlantic, it was part of a far greater national conflict of ideas, ambitions and administrative systems, and had repercussions far beyond the events of which it was composed. In France, doubts about the capabilities of the French navy were reinforced and, coinciding with military success on its land frontiers, may have helped settle the future direction of French policy. Although the arrival of the convoy was a morale victory for the republic, it was the simultaneous defeat of the allied armies on the Belgian frontier and the subsequent advance of the French armies to the Rhine that was the real morale booster of the summer which ensured the republic's survival. For France a naval victory would have been useful but a land victory was really immediately necessary, whereas British reactions showed that their priorities were perhaps the reverse. In Britain the victory reinforced confidence to press ahead with grand plans to dismantle the French colonial empire and to cut up French naval power root and branch. It provided encouragement to continue fighting despite defeats on the continent. The battle accordingly had its place in the evolution of the war. Both in its immediate gains and losses in ships and men which bore heavily on the seafaring communities in both France and Britain, and in its artistic and material legacy which influenced the way succeeding generations viewed it, it also had an impact on morale and national consciousness that affected longer-term relations between France and Britain. Within the prevailing environments in those adjacent communities, the battle contributed to long-term perceptions of each other as a maritime power—perceptions that affected both the conduct of two further decades of war in Europe and two centuries of international relations.[17]

Notes

1. P. Jupp (ed.), *The Letter Journal of George Canning, 1793–1795* (Camden Fourth Series, vol. 41, London, 1991) p. 121.
2. *The Times*, 12 June 1794 p. 2; J. Stevenson, *Popular Disturbances in England 1700–1832* (London, 1992) p. 208.
3. B. Turnstall (ed. N. Tracy), *Naval Warfare in the Age of Sail* (London, 1990) p. 210; E. Taillemite, *L'Histoire ignore de la marine française* (Paris, 1988) p. 283; M. Acerra and J. Meyer, *Marines et Révolution* (Rennes, 1988) p. 178.
4. N. Hampson, *La Marine de l'an II: mobilisation de la flotte de l'Océan 1793–1794* (Paris, 1959); W.S. Cormack, *Revolution and Political Conflict in the French Navy 1789–1794* (Cambridge, 1995) Ch. 9.
5. Cormack, op. cit., p. 276 n. 141.
6. Hampson, op. cit., pp. 86–87.
7. In addition to the eyewitness accounts published here, British Library Add Mss 23207 and Public Record Office ADM1/100

contain accounts of the actions of their own ships drawn up by Howe's captains at his request. Thirty-three log and journal accounts were published in 1899 by the Navy Records Society in *Logs of the Great Sea Fights 1794–1805*, edited by T. Sturges Jackson. Two by the second and third lieutenants of the *Brunswick*, Rowland Bevan and William Kemble, were published in 1928 by the Navy Records Society in *The Naval Miscellany*, vol. 3, edited by W. Perrin. Hugh Owen has printed the account by Midshipman Joseph Thompson of the *Barfleur* in *The Mariner's Mirror*, vol. 80 (1994) pp. 335–8. Oliver Warner used a number of other accounts in writing his book *The Glorious First of June* (London, 1961).

8. *The Times*, 14 June 1794 p. 2.

9. Moreau de Jonnès, *Adventures in the Revolution and under the Consulate* (London, 1969) p. 73.

10. *The Times*, 14 June 1794.

11. Dundas to the prime minister, William Pitt, 9 July 1794, printed in A. Aspinall and E. Anthony Smith (eds), *English Historical Documents 1783–1832* (London, 1959) p. 124; for Howe's Instuctions see Appendix to Ware's article below.

12. P. Jarnoux, 'Autour des combats de Prairal: Le convoi Van Stabel et les approvisionnements Americans en 1793–1794' in *Les marines française et britannique face aux Etats-Unis (1776–1865)* (Vincennes, Service historique de la marine, 2000), 183–84.

13. Jarnoux, 'Autour des combats de Prairal', 182–83; *The Times*, 7 July 1794; PRO ADM2/1347 Admiralty to Howe 14 June 1794; W. James, *The Naval History of Great Britain* (London, 1837), vol. 1, p. 122.

14. *The Times*, 12 June 1794; James, *Naval History*, vol. 1, p. 182.

15. The origins of the name given to the battle are also discussed by Hugh Owen in 'An eyewitness account of the Glorious First of June 1794', *Mariner's Mirror*, vol. 80, p. 336.

16. Published in *Les marines française et britannique face aux Etats-Unis (1776–1865)*, pp. 155–67.

17. The editors wish to acknowledge their debt to Pieter van der Merwe for his part in the production of this volume, to Hugh Owen for documentary material he unselfishly supplied as a result of the discussion at the Conference, and to Mike Rouillard for redrawing the charts used here to illustrate the operations.

2

The Prairial Battles
The French Viewpoint

André Delaporte

The 'Prairial' battles between the French and British fleets in June 1794 took place at a critical time and against a very difficult background for France. It was at a critical time because the battles came two years after the Girondins' declaration of war against the crowned heads of Europe, and little more than one year after the beginning of war against England, just before the ninth of Thermidor (27 July).[1] The context was one in which revolutionary France was in great difficulties because she was threatened on all fronts, inside and out, simultaneously engaged on the continent and at sea where she was once more in conflict with Britain. The critical time and difficult background were compounded at the end of spring 1794 by a serious food supply crisis which could have been fatal to the young republic; hence the need to call on imports of food and colonial products from the United States of America. This was the mission assigned to Rear Admiral Vanstabel.[2]

Vanstabel's mission

During the previous winter, Rear Admiral Vanstabel had mustered a convoy of more than a hundred French and American merchant ships laden with a great number of different products but predominantely carrying wheat flour. Escorted by warships, this convoy left the United States of America on the twenty-eighth of Germinal (17 April), second year of the Republic (1794). On the third of Floréal (22 April); a despatch vessel arrived at Brest from Vanstabel announcing that he would probably arrive about the fifteenth of Floréal (4 May).

The plan of naval operations had been fixed on the sixth, seventh and eighth of Pluviôse (25–27 January). The fleet under the orders of Rear Admiral Villaret-Joyeuse included three squadrons of three divisions each. With the aim of an expedition against Jersey, one division of eight ships of the line and six frigates under Rear Admiral Cornic was detached into Cancale. Another division under Rear Admiral Nielly of five of the line, two frigates and a corvettte was ordered to meet Vanstabel's convoy. After the cancellation of the expedition to Jersey—having been delayed by continuous westerly winds—it was only on the twenty-first of Germinal (10 April) that Nielly was able to sail with his five battleships.[3]

Learning of the anticipated arrival of the convoy, the French Minister for the navy, Dalbarade, wrote to Rear Admiral Villaret-Joyeuse (hereafter Villaret) on the seventh of Floréal (26 April): 'The intention of the Committee of Public Safety is for the fleet to get under way to join Nielly and Vanstabel with the Cancale division, if the enemy itself gets under way. But in that case, the safety of the convoy will be its only objective, the only rule of conduct of the commander of the fleet.'[4] This letter—in fact a preparatory order—shows that engagement with the enemy should not be sought at all costs, but that the safety of the convoy had at all times to be its first preoccupation. On the twenty-seventh of Floréal (16 May), the Committee of Public Safety confirmed the previous instructions: to get underway only if the convoy ran a risk, and if the coming of the English navy was absolutely certain:

> We must not compromise our naval forces when all our supplementary means are not yet put into execution and when the smallest failure could halt our plan of campaign against England . . . it is not a naval victory we need at the moment, but our convoy; it is not a battle but a proud and imposing

posture which will ward off the enemy or make it to hove to. To delay our revenge is to make it more sure.[5]

So it was understood that everything had to be done to save the convoy, but nevertheless to keep forces in reserve for the next action against Britain. The fleet had to protect the convoy but without taking unnecessary risks; and Dalbarade speculates on the nature of the intimidation that was necessary to make Admiral Howe give up the struggle. One can understand the difficulties of interpretation that faced Villaret and the government's political representative with the fleet, Jeanbon Saint-André, on reading this text. Indeed, there was only one means of warding off the threat that the enemy placed over the convoy: it was to destroy their fleet. But the Committee of Public Safety was certainly conscious, in spite of the efforts of Jeanbon Saint-André (hereafter Jeanbon) for 'regenerating' the republican navy, of the inadequacies in material, in personnel, in staff, in training: a direct confrontation might be fatal to the French fleet.

It is obvious that these orders had the effect of restricting Villaret's freedom of action. He tried to avoid a serious engagement. As he put it, he let his movements depend on those of the British fleet: therefore, his manoeuvres were guided by Howe's. In fact, during the three fights of ninth, tenth and thirteenth of Prairial (28, 29 May and 1 June), the tactical initiative was constantly to belong to the British.

The Prairial fights

On the twenty-seventh of Floréal, in the second year of the Republic (16 May 1794), on a fine but foggy day, the French fleet left the Brest roadstead. Two days later, Villaret learned that Vanstabel had left the Chesapeake on about 10 April. Then, the next day, a prize permitted the fleet to learn that the enemy was underway. Jeanbon's orders were to join up with Nielly's division, which evidently had not yet met Vanstabel's convoy. From the first to the ninth of Prairial (20–28 May), the French fleet cruised between forty-six and forty-eight degrees of latitude in search of Nielly. Eventually he would be found, but too late for that effort to procure for the French fleet a numerical advantage.

For it was on the ninth of Prairial (28 May) at 8 a.m. that a great number of sails appeared in the south-east. Villaret and Jeanbon thought first that it was the convoy. But only one hour later the ships were identified as those of the enemy.

At the end of the first day of fighting, the French and the British seem to have made equal play: on both sides, one vessel was badly damaged and put back to port. The French casualty was the 110-gun *Révolutionnaire* one of the most beautiful of Villaret's fleet. The tactical advantage, however, stayed on the British side, which did not want to release its prey, the French fleet. As for Villaret, he manoeuvred deliberately to avoid fighting: he looked to escape, in accordance with the orders of the Committee of Public Safety.

During next day, the tenth of Prairial (29 May), we see the admiral manoeuvring well enough to rescue his rear squadron when it was in danger. In fact, he had been caught by the enemy. During the morning Villaret did not want to go into action, even though he had the opportunity. He allowed his advanced squadron to get damaged and lost one vessel (the *Montagnard*, which limped away and was picked up by Vanstabel three days later), he let his rear squadron get damaged and lost another vessel (the *Indomptable*, towed away from the fleet by a frigate), and finally he lost the advantage of the wind and with it his full freedom of action. Between four and five o'clock in the afternoon, Villaret had a second opportunity to engage, but he allowed himself to be intimidated from doing so.

On the eleventh of Prairial (30 May) in the morning, Nielly reinforced Villaret with the three ships he still had with him (*Sans Pareil, Trajan, Téméraire*[6]). As Jeanbon and Villaret knew, they were being chased by the British, so that they planned to draw the enemy into the north and west in order that the convoy might sail twenty-five leagues to the south of both fleets. At 8.30 a.m. on the thirteenth of Prairial (1 June), Lord Howe raised his signal: he ordered each vessel to move independently and to engage its opponent in the enemy line. From 9.30 a.m., the battle became extremely confused and looked like a series of single combats. Failures occurred in the French line. Some vessels left the line and let themselves drift, which allowed the British vessels to form into groups against individual French ships: three against Bouvet's *Terrible*; two, then three, against the *Juste*; four against the *Achille*; the *Brunswick* and the *Ramilies* against the *Vengeur du Peuple*; the *Queen Charlotte*, the *Gibraltar*, the *Culloden* against the *Montagne*, Villaret's flagship.

At the end of that day, when the failures were to be attributed to the cowardice of some and to the dismasting shots practised by the British, Villaret left seven vessels to the enemy: the *Achille*, the *Sans Pareil*, the *Northumberland*, the *Juste*, the *Impétueux*, the *America* and the *Vengeur du Peuple* which sank at the same time as the *Culloden* took possession of her. Villaret could doubtless have started fighting again. But at 8 p.m., he steered for Brest with nineteen vessels, five of them dismasted like pontoons. The republican fleet was no longer disturbed by Lord Howe who, with his six prizes, sailed for Portsmouth where he arrived on 13 June. So, if he had a victory, it was a limited one. Indeed, the true victory would have consisted in the destruction of the enemy fleet: but neither one nor the other of the opponents gained that kind of victory at the end of the battle of the thirteenth of Prairial.

An analysis of the conflict shows that Vanstabel's convoy was the main stake. On the British side, the aim was to take possession of it; on the French side, to drive such danger away from it. If Villaret looked as if he would exceed the orders of his government, hooking the British vanguard in the morning of the tenth, it was because he seemed to have wanted at all costs to distract British attention from the course of the convoy. Indeed, if Howe had avoided the fight and sent his ships after the convoy, he might have succeeded in destroying it. Public opinion on both sides of Channel seemed to forget the existence of the convoy. Villaret was reproached in France for having shown no offensive spirit, for having been out-manoeuvred and then defeated. In Britain Lord Howe was reproached for not having made capital out of his victory by destroying the republican fleet.

Analysis of Villaret-Joyeuse's behaviour

Criticism from a strict military viewpoint of the behaviour of the French fleet during the Prairial fighting has focused on mistakes in the orders of the Committee of Public Safety. For instance, the

Cancale division only joined up with the main French fleet when it returned to Brest after the departure of the English fleet; Rear Admiral Cornic was unable to unite before and the six vessels of his division were missed bitterly at the time of the battle. The same kind of mistake sent Rear Admiral Nielly's squadron in quest of Vanstabel's convoy: Nielly's squadron did not find the convoy, and when Nielly rejoined the main part of the fleet in the morning of the eleventh of Prairial (30 May), he could do nothing but fill up the gaps which had been made during the two previous days, and then it was too late. The separate dispatch of these two divisions of the French fleet were big military mistakes. They had the effect of dispersing naval forces precisely at the time the French feared the interception of the Vanstabel's convoy.

The orders of the Committee of Public Safety were also criticized for being ambiguous. They specified indeed that, in the event of an encounter, a naval victory was unnecessary for the time being; it was sufficient just to intimidate the enemy enough to persuade him to give up his plans. So, directing Villaret to maintain his forces on the defensive and suggesting he should sacrifice the immediate possibility (the destruction of Howe's fleet) for a future one (a later plan of invasion of England), the Committee of Public Safety deprived itself of control of the sea, which could have resulted from the offensive behaviour of a concentrated fleet that resolutely swooped down upon its prey. Villaret was only allowed to behave—metaphorically speaking— like a sheep dog or a guard dog of the convoy. He was not allowed to behave like a hound, even if he was able to show his teeth and to bite when attacked. Critics who reproach Villaret for not having acted like a hound deceive themselves. He had all the more to keep to his guarding role, as the political shepherd himself, Jeanbon, was on board with him. Jeanbon prided himself on naval knowledge and was there to watch over the performance of the orders of the Committee of Public Safety. The Committee thought that Vanstabel's convoy was absolutely vital for France in general and for the revolution in particular. An attack on the British fleet was not absolutely guaranteed to achieve success. Furthermore, if it failed, it could give control of the sea to Lord Howe who could seize Vanstabel's convoy and decisively compromise the hopes of revenge which the Committee of Public Safety nourished against England.

So we may note that, on this occasion, the Committee of Public Safety showed a certain pragmatism, doubtless conscious of the inferiority of the French fleet in relation to the Royal Navy. In contrast to the aggressive rantings which usually spouted from the tribune of the Convention, this nearly secret pragmatism, in the form of personal orders to Villaret, proved effectual. Under the protection of its guard dog (Villaret), the flock (Vanstabel's convoy) arrived complete into the fold (the harbour). But this pragmatism, effective as it was, was neither glorious nor conformed to the martial accents of the current Montagnards' speeches: indeed, the sheep dog came home crippled and wounded. People began to mock or to be furious about it. They noticed the pitiful state of the fleet after the battle, and were astonished at the absence of seven vessels. In their declarations, Villaret and Jeanbon emphasized that their operations had been fully in accordance with the aim of avoiding famine in France through the safe arrival of the food convoy. This was explained by Jeanbon in the session of sixteenth Messidor (4 July) of the Convention: 'Perhaps you will see like me a great political victory in a military reverse: for the objective of the two fleets was the convoy, and that which protected it from the rapacious tooth of the English leopard, you will doubtless judge is also that which has best fulfilled the views of its government.'[7]

Thus it must be well understood that opinion on the Prairial battles was perverted from the beginning by considerations of personal or domestic policy. Personal considerations: indeed, if it was evident that, on the thirteenth of Prairial, some captains did not perform their duty, it was easy for the accused to put the responsibility for the losses on their Admiral. The way in which some and not others were treated shows that favouritism also played a powerful part. This way of paying off old scores was not at all to be neglected, just as it was in the interest of Villaret and Jeanbon, doubtless conscious of their own deficiencies, to stay together to produce the same version of events, that one that prevailed in the end.

Of course, considerations of domestic policy played a part too. Just as Jeanbon and Villaret emphasized that they had achieved their aim, the whole of anti-revolutionary Europe backing Britain, as well as royalists and federalists in France, emphasized the defeat of the republican fleet. For the British, the First of June was a 'Glorious' day. On the French side, even if it had really been a strategic success, the arrival of a merchant convoy could not raise itself to the level of glory of a naval victory. But the terrorist government in France, which had no more than several weeks to live, needed to raise the prestige of the revolution in France and in the rest of Europe. This is the reason why, when the end of the *Vengeur du Peuple* was known, Barère— as spokesman of the Committee of Public Safety—got hold of it at once to produce a republican propaganda monument. Paradoxically, his picture of the martyred vessel had the effect of emphasizing the appearance of a French defeat as a result of the Prairial battles.

Fulfilled mission

The 'so much desired arrival' from America of Vanstabel's convoy of 'one hundred and twenty four sails, including the prizes' took place on the twenty-sixth of Prairial (14 June).[8] The objective fixed by the Convention, to which Villaret and Jeanbon had been subjected, had thus been attained. In pursuit of these orders, Villaret had not ceased 'to move the enemy away from the course it [the convoy] had to steer'. He did not approach the British fleet to engage in battle, but he made every effort to move it as far away as he could from the supposed course of Vanstabel's convoy.

The convoy came safely into port, undamaged and swollen with the addition of sixteen prizes. Villaret's tactics corresponded with the strategy ordered by the Committee of Public Safety. From a strategic point of view, it was a victory: not only did the convoy come into port, but further, if at the end of fighting (which Villaret did not deliberately seek) the French fleet had been soundly thrashed, it had not been destroyed and remained ready for later operations against Britain in compliance with the orders of the Committee of Public Safety. During the whole battle, Villaret behaved like a guard dog, both before and after the fighting: before in going out to meet the convoy; after in keeping at a distance Montagu's squadron (twenty-first of Prairial) which cruised off Ushant and did not try to become involved in the fighting. During the days of ninth, tenth and thirteenth of Prairial, he behaved like a lure to incite the British fleet to follow him in order to draw it away from the convoy. To this end, he succeeded perfectly even if, all things considered, he suffered severe losses.

Afterwards, he was blamed for reasons which are indeed contradictory: some held that he had exceeded the orders of the Committee of Public Safety by giving battle to the Royal Navy; but that criticism looks fallacious when others, on the opposite tack, reproach him with having fled from Lord Howe and with having made up his mind to fight only when it became impossible to avoid it. He was also blamed for having missed several favourable opportunities; in short, for not having shown an offensive spirit. Behaving as he did, Villaret abode by the letter of the Convention's orders, even if it can retrospectively be deplored that he was unable to display tactical initiatives on the tenth and thirteenth of Prairial (29 May and 1 June) which might perhaps have turned the situation in his favour and given the republic a tactical victory in addition to the strategic victory.

It was with the jubilation of a revolutionary festival that, on the twenty-second of Prairial, the fleet was welcomed into the Berthaume roadstead. The subsequent writings of Villaret, Jeanbon and the Committee of Public Safety are unanimous in celebrating the victory constituted by the arrival of the convoy at Brest, even if they express regret at not having destroyed the British fleet on this occasion which would have given the Convention control of the sea and thus world command. According to Villaret, the fault lay in the inexperience and the incompetence of some captains, the cowardice of some seamen, the skill of the English gunners, their use of chain shot and carronades, as well as the failure of some French vessels to observe signals, and the inexperience of insufficiently trained crews, a large part of which were formed from fishermen, volunteers and soldiers from the army.

From justification to propaganda

At this time of the war, both France and Britain had an interest in believing or convincing themselves that they had won the day. Britain claimed that a thrashing had been inflicted on the fleet of the young republic to such an extent that the Royal Navy henceforth held naval supremacy. France claimed that not only had Vanstabel's convoy been saved, but that its fleet had been little-damaged and was ready to free the seas from the yoke of English tyranny, as Jeanbon declaimed at the tribune of the Jacobin Club.

There were also domestic and foreign policy viewpoints. The Montagnard-dominated Convention, then in its last weeks, had to make up an official story to counter the rumours which were disseminated by the English press, and in France by opponents of the Robespierrist regime, that the revolutionary fleet had suffered a great disaster. To thwart this enemy propaganda, it was necessary to project the sacrificial aspect of the Prairial fights. This is what Jeanbon and Barère tried to do at the Convention, the former saying that the sacrifice of Villaret's vessels and crews had allowed the convoy to reach Brest. Barère, embroidering on English newspaper reports with his inimitable bombastic grandiloquence, made up the legend of the *Vengeur du Peuple* during the session of the twenty-first of Messidor. This myth was hard to eradicate during the nineteenth century and survived into the twentieth century. We can still find traces of it in some French school books between the two last wars. Then came the easy *hypercritique*, making fun of Captain Renaudin feasting on mutton pâté on the *Culloden* with Lieutenant Griffiths at the time when he had been described as sinking heroically with his vessel.

Revision of these myths has been relatively recent. During the 'Sea Day' at Brest in May 1994, Professor Alain Boulaire proved clearly that Renaudin, former master in the French merchant navy, did not behave so badly during the battle. Philippe Henwood and Edmond Monange think that, after all, the seamen of the *Vengeur du Peuple* were not unworthy either of their glory or of their legend. Jacques Gury has also spoken about a real poetic wreck, meticulously studying poetic and musical works composed on the occasion of the shipwreck of the *Vengeur du Peuple* at

Barère's instigation. Poetic wreck had two meanings: first, that the myth was nothing but 'a heap of commonplaces' in the antique taste and 'empty ranting rhetoric' after the manner of the eighteenth century; secondly and paradoxically, that it was due to these poets and their bombastic odes that the result of the Prairial battle was undervalued, because they claimed that a bloody sacrifice was better altogether than a half-victory. This so focused attention on the wreck of the *Vengeur du Peuple* that they temporarily concealed the real achievement of the republican fleet: the preservation of the convoy.

These recent considerations confirm the relevant remark written by Jacques Bordenove: that though the loss of seven vessels was a serious reverse for the republican fleet, Howe had doubly failed, as he neither succeeded in destroying the naval power of the Republic, nor in capturing Vanstabel's convoy, which was a considerable tactical failure in view of Britain's command of the sea. Finally, after the lessons of Second World War, historians' considerations at last corroborate those of the military: for indeed, though the allied convoys suffered incessant attacks from the German Navy which inflicted losses on them, nobody would now assert that their coming into port was a defeat. All this explains why French historians of today have reverted to the appreciation formerly given by Villaret and Jeanbon before the Convention, that they did nothing but carry out their orders.

Notes

1. The date of the coup in Paris which led to the fall of Robespierre and the end of the 'Reign of Terror'.
2. Pierre-Jean Vanstabel, born at Dunkirk 1744. Formerly an officer in the *Compagnie des Indes*. He distinguished himself in the War of American Independence as an auxiliary officer in the French Navy to which he transferred finally in 1792. In January 1793 he was promoted to captain and after a successful period as a commerce raider in the frigate *Thétis*, became captain of the 74-gun *Tigre* and was one of the few commanders who maintained discipline among his crew in the Quiberon mutiny in September, probably occasioning his promotion to rear admiral. He quickly

distinguished himself by a foray in command of a squadron in November 1793 when he successfully evaded Howe's fleet and returned to Brest with eleven prizes. He died at Dunkirk in 1797.

3. These were *Sans Pareil, Trajan, Téméraire, Patriote* and *Audacieux*.
4. Quoted in G. Bordonnove, *Les Marins de l'An II* (Paris, 1974) p. 165.
5. *Receuil des actes du comitéde Salut public avec la correspondence officielle des représentants en mission et le registre du Conseil exécutif provisoire* (Paris, 1901) vol. 13, pp. 441–42.
6. The *Patriote* had become separated and joined Villaret's fleet on 19 May. *Audacieux* had also separated and on 29 May found the damaged *Révolutionnaire* which it towed to Rochefort.
7. As reported in the *Moniteur universal*, no. 287, septidi 17 Messidor, l'An II (Saturday 5 July 1794).
8. I have earlier purposely described the convoy as 'more than a hundred' because so many sources diverge concerning the exact number which formed Vanstabel's convoy. According to different texts it was a matter of 110, 116, 124, 127, 130 even 170 vessels. This last figure, extremely exaggerated (but still exceeded by Lamartine who spoke of '200 ships loaded with wheat' [*Histoire des Girondins*]), was given by Vanstabel's widow to obtain a pension from the Consulate and then from Napoleon (Vanstabel dossier, Archives de la Marine, Vincennes). A letter of 26 Prairial, year 2 (Archives marines F. 182, Archives Nationales) speaks of 'the arrival in our port [Brest] of the so much desired convoy from America. It amounts to 124 sail including prizes'. In the Vanstabel dossier in the Archives de la Marine at Vincennes can be found the list of 'Prizes taken by the Division under the orders of Rear-admiral Vanstabel, leaving from Chesapeake Bay, 28 Germinal, year 2 of the Republic, with the Grand Convoy composed of 116 sail, arrived at the port of Brest, 20 Prairial'. The count of prizes reaches sixteen. If the convoy is added this provides a total of 132, and if the ships of the naval squadron are also added (two of the line, four frigates, four corvettes and two storeships) it ends up as 144—different figures again from all those previously mentioned.

Sources and bibliography

Archives de la Marine and Bibliothèques du Service Historique de la Marine, at Vincennes, Brest, Rochefort, Paris.
Archives de la Marine at the Archives nationales: BB 4 36: croisières

dans la Manche, division de Cancale; BB 4 37: armée navale de Brest, C.-A. Villaret-Joyeuse, combats de prairial An II; BB 4 39 dossiers de bâtiments. Affaire du *Vengeur du Peuple*. G. Troude, *Batailles navales de la France* (Paris, 1868) vols 2 and 3.

L. Lévy-Schneider, *Le Conventionnel Jeanbon Saint-André* (Paris, 1901).

L. Nicolas, *La puissance navale dans l'Histoire* (Paris, 1958).

Philippe Masson, *Histoire des batailles navales de la voile aux missiles* (Paris, 1983).

Jean Ducros, 'Les combats de prairial et l'arrivée à bon port du convoi de Van Stabel', in *Cols bleus*, no. 2263 (11 June 1994).

Georges Bordonove, *Les marins de l'An II* (Paris, 1974).

G. Barbotin, *Étude documentaire sur le combat de prairial an II, l'épisode du Vengeur* (Rochefort, 1930).

Alain Boulaire and Edmond Monange, '*Le Vengeur du Peuple*; réalité, fiction, naissance d'un mythe', in *Populations et Cultures, Études réunies en l'honneur de François Lebrun* (Rennes, 1989).

Philippe Henwood and Edmond Monange, *Brest, un port en révolution, 1789–1799* (Rennes, 1989).

Capitaine de Corvette Antoine, *Les combats de Prairial*, in *Travaux historiques de l'Ecole de Guerre navale (1920–1937), sujets antérieurs à 1914* (Paris, 1921).

Pascale Ferchaud, *L'épisode tragique du Vengeur, histoire et légende* (édité par la Société d'histoire et d'archéologie en Saintonge maritime, Marennes, 1995).

Recent exhibitions or memorials

Symposium at Brest, Saturday 14 May 1994, with papers by Alain Boulaire, Jacques Gury, Edmond Monange et Yves Tripier, organized by the Service Historique de la Marine à Brest and the Société d'Études de Brest et du Léon.

Le Gua (Charente Maritime), exposition sur *le Vengeur du Peuple*, 16–31 August 1994.

3

The Glorious First of June
The British Strategic Perspective

Christopher Ware

The war which came about as a consequence of the revolution in France in 1789 was to be different from others in what has been called 'The Second Hundred Years War'. Based as it was on ideological grounds rather than dynastic pretensions of European monarchies, it unleashed powerful and destabilizing forces. The fear that the revolutionary infection would cross the Channel added to the normal fear of invasion which seemed perennial throughout the wars of the eighteenth century.

The threat of invasion was again in the air in 1794. In June 1793, the ruling French Committee of Public Safety had developed ambitious plans to expand its fleet from the sixty-five ships of the line and about seventy-eight frigates at the start of the war to one hundred of the line and 127 frigates. In the spring it had contemplated attacking the Channel Islands and by late September it was projecting using its growing navy to support the transport of an army of 100,000 men against Britain for which it began to assemble barges and coastal craft. Early 1794 saw the assembly of 20,000 men, 154 transports, six ships of the line, two rasées and five frigates at Cancale on the north coast of Brittany, preparatory for the first step: the occupation of the Channel Islands.[1] In February 1794 the British government authorized the formation of local volunteer defence units, but its main defence against invasion was as always its Channel Fleet. Among the objects to which the Admiralty directed Lord Howe in April, as he prepared the Channel Fleet for sea, he was to bear 'always in mind that a due regard to the Security of the Kingdoms of Great Britain and Ireland must ever form one of the most essential and constant Objects of your care and attention'. He was also to take under his direction Admiral Macbride's squadron which had the specific task of covering the Channel Islands against the threatened attack. Howe's Instructions are appended as Document 3.i, on page 43.

The need to guard against invasion was a tiresome diversion of British attention from the grand strategy envisaged by the war minister of Pitt's government, Henry Dundas. He saw two essential British objectives from the war: the expansion of British commerce and the destruction of French sea power. Both were to be ensured by a massive expedition to the West Indies, the rich economic heart of the French colonial empire. Always an object of British expeditions in eighteenth-century wars, the Caribbean was to see troops, men and ships dedicated to this conquest in unprecedented numbers. This principal thrust was, however, part of an interconnected wider plan which he outlined to a fellow Scot, Sir Gilbert Elliot in September 1793. The latter recorded that:

> Dundas showed me the force intended for the West Indies under Sir Charles Grey. It is upwards of 17,000 men on paper. He says they are to sail in October, and that with such a force they cannot fail of taking all the French islands; that Martinico and St Domingo may be attacked at the same time; that part of this force will be brought back to Gibraltar in the spring in time to go on an expedition against Toulon, for which he hopes to have 50,000 men ready, including 6,000 Neapolitans— Austrians, Sardinians, British, Hessians, etc. that with this force the capture and demolition of Toulon may be depended upon; that there will be [an]other 50,000 men ready to attack Brest, and that he trusts our fleet will in the meanwhile strike some decisive blow against this navy; that after such a blow to the French naval power the capture of the West Indian islands will prevent there restoring it, and this he states as the

principal object proposed by the war in favour of Great Britain as a compensation for our charge in it.[2]

The general war strategy was thus to inflict immediate material damage on the French navy by defeating it at sea and destroying its arsenals, while capturing its colonies (so expanding British commerce and destroying that of the French) so as to prevent any future French naval recovery to be again the formidable rival that it had been in the previous War of American Independence.[3] Wars, however, seldom work out to a designed timetable and one consequence when unexpected events happened was that there were to be insufficient forces available to take advantage of them. The first of these occurred in August 1793 when a British squadron under Lord Hood was invited into Toulon, the principal French Mediterranean naval base. In conjunction with her allies, the Spanish and Sardinians, Britain tried to retain the enclave as a base to destabilize the south of France. There was even tentative discussion concerning the establishment of Monsieur (eldest brother of the executed Louis XVI) as ruler of the area and effecting a Bourbon restoration.[4] All of these plans came to nothing, based as they were on a misunderstanding of the true state of the south of France and the fact that the major offensive effort was already determined to be in the West Indies, so that only three ships of the line and part of the Gibraltar garrison were diverted to Toulon. Thus, by the close of 1793 the British had the first opportunity to strike at French naval power but had been unwilling and, to an extent, unable to redirect resources to support the operations at Toulon.

The inability to grasp at such opportunities was primarily the result of military rather than naval limitations. Britain lacked large reserves of trained soldiers. The material state of the navy was probably better at the start of this conflict than at the start of any earlier war in the century. Recent research has shown that the Royal Navy came out of the War of American Independence with investment in building and repair at very high levels and that this was to continue during the short peace.[5] This in turn meant that mobilization of the fleet went ahead more smoothly than in past wars when defects had had to be rectified before the full potential of the navy could be realized. That this was in no small part due to the First Lord of the Admiralty during the American war, the Earl of Sandwich, has been persuasively argued by Dr Rodger in his recent biography of Sandwich.[6] Better prepared, the Royal Navy soon established supremacy in the Channel and Western Approaches. The French navy was still disrupted by effects of the revolution on its arsenals and on the manning of the fleet, including the defection of much of its royalist officer corps. Moreover in the summer of 1793 it was preoccupied with establishing a *cordon sanitaire* in the Bay of Biscay between the Vendéean royalist rebels of south-western France and any possible assistance to them from Britain. The Channel Fleet and its frigate squadrons performed one of their essential functions in protecting the commerce of Britain and its allies and clearing that of France from the seas in the first year of the war.

In fact this created a further unexpected complication when the neutral Baltic powers reacted angrily to the British claim to a right to search their vessels for French property and contraband of war, and in March 1794 Sweden persuaded Denmark into a joint convention to protect their ships from insult and they took steps to arm sixteen ships of the line to enforce this Armed Neutrality. The danger that this might extend across the Atlantic, and become something worse, then arose when the British West Indies expedition arrived in the Caribbean and prize-hungry naval captains began snapping up merchantmen trading with the French islands. Since in order to maintain their commerce in wartime the French opened their colonial trade to neutral ships this at once brought Britain into conflict with the leading neutral interloper in the Caribbean, the United States of America, which reacted by imposing a temporary embargo on trade with Britain and its colonies and threatened to raise an army of 50,000 men. Moderates managed to prevent hostilities going any further while an envoy was sent to Britain to negotiate on the issues in dispute between the two countries, but the Swedish envoy in London approached the American envoy with a view to the United States joining the northern Armed Neutrality.

Part of the problem which the neutrals could exploit was the lack of a decisive result to the war at sea, for despite the expectations of the anxious British public the Channel Fleet failed to bring the French Atlantic fleet to action and strike the

*Fig. 3.i. Richard, Earl Howe, Admiral of the Fleet (1726–99),
by John Singleton Copley (1737–1815). NMM BHC2790.*

'decisive blow against this navy' that war minister Dundas
wanted. For all its better state of preparation the Royal Navy still
had something to prove. Dr Rodger has argued that all navies
suffer a kind of ring rust when they have not seen major action for
some time, and that their effectiveness increases (or diminishes) as
time goes on throughout the war, depending upon the outcome
of the actions in which they engage. Effectiveness in action was
the more uncertain for the Royal Navy on this occasion because
its officer corps was still suffering the after-effects of the political
splits that had riven it during the preceding war. The British
fleet in home waters was commanded by an admiral who had

helped cause this split, Admiral Earl Howe (see Fig. 3.i). Some officers had not spoken to him for several years prior to the outbreak of the war.[7] The fleet needed to be tested and tempered in battle.

In fact the fleet had already helped initiate the process by which the pieces were put in place that were to lead to the long awaited major battle in 1794. Forced out of the West Indies by the British offensive and shut off from reaching France by British dominance of the Channel and Western Approaches, a large number of valuable French West Indiamen laden with sugar and coffee sought refuge in the ports of the eastern seaboard of the United States where they waited for a naval escort to convoy them safely home. They thus constituted the valuable cash-crop nucleus of Vanstabel's convoy to protect which the French fleet exposed itself to attack on the Glorious First of June.

Until June 1794 the operations of the British home fleet followed a well-worn pattern. The bigger ships of the line, the first and second rates, spent the winter in port, while the third rates and frigates had kept the seas to watch for movements out of the French Atlantic ports of Brest and Rochefort. Lord Howe was sent his instructions on 17 April (see Document 3.i on page 43) setting out his tasks. He was to cover the passage down Channel of the outward bound convoys to the East and West Indies and to Newfoundland. He was to make a detachment from his fleet which, having seen the trade safely out, was to search for 'a very large and valuable Fleet of Merchant ships' coming to France from America. He was to station himself to protect British and allied trade entering or leaving the Channel and to intercept French warships, privateers and trade, bearing in mind also the need to ensure the security of the British Isles.[8]

Howe sailed with the fleet to cover the trades on their outward bound voyage from St Helens road (between Portsmouth and the Isle of Wight) on 2 May 1794. There were 148 vessels in all, made up of 99 merchant ships and 49 ships of war. Thirty-four were ships of the line (including a 74 and a 64 going all the way to India).[9] By 4 May the fleet and its charges had reached the Lizard where Howe detached Rear Admiral Montagu with six 74s and three frigates to take the trades as far as the latitude of Cape Finisterre (see Fig. 3.ii). He was then to search for the homeward

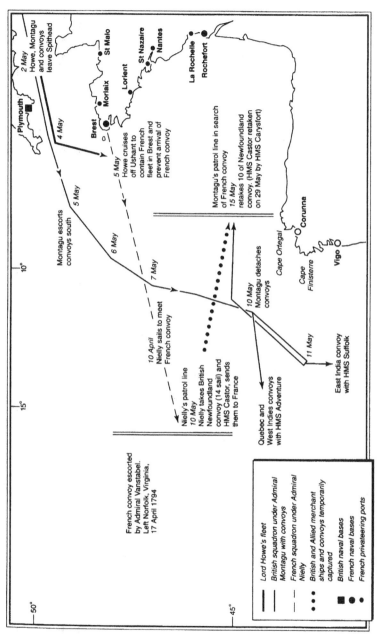

Fig. 3.ii. Chart of operations 10 April–15 May 1794.

French convoy escorted by Admiral Vanstabel. Left Norfolk, Virginia, 17 April 1794

2 May Howe, Montagu and convoys leave Spithead

4 May

5 May
Montagu escorts convoys south

6 May

7 May

10 April
Nielly sails to meet French convoy

Nielly's patrol line
10 May
Nielly takes British Newfoundland convoy (14 sail) and HMS Castor, sends them to France

Quebec and West Indies convoys with HMS Adventure

East India convoy with HMS Suffolk

10 May
Montagu detaches convoys

Montagu's patrol line in search of French convoy
15 May
retakes 10 of Newfoundland convoy. (HMS Castor retaken on 29 May by HMS Carysfort)

5 May
Howe cruises off Ushant to contain French fleet in Brest and prevent arrival of French convoy

Plymouth

Brest

Morlaix
St Malo

Lorient

St Nazaire
Nantes

La Rochelle
Rochefort

Cape Ortegal

Corunna

Cape Finisterre

Vigo

50°

45°

15°

10°

Lord Howe's fleet

British squadron under Admiral Montagu with convoys

French squadron under Admiral Nielly

British and Allied merchant ships and convoys temporarily captured

British naval bases

French naval bases

French privateering ports

31

bound French convoy. Howe, having fulfilled the first part of his instructions, shaped course to Ushant, the station of the Western Squadrons from the 1740s to the 1760s. Having sent cruisers in to survey Brest and ascertained that the French fleet was still in port, he then quartered the Bay of Biscay, returning off Ushant on 18 May. The next day he sent two more frigates to check on the French fleet. On this reconnaissance, however, he found the road empty: the French, having been alerted by his previous visit, had sent all available warships out to cover the arrival of the convoy from America on the 16 May, passing Howe's returning fleet in dense fog on the May 17.[10] Not for the first time they had slipped past a watching British fleet.

The French had earlier sent Rear Admiral Nielly with one 80- and four 74-gun ships of the line, three frigates and a corvette to meet the incoming convoy of 117 merchantmen loaded with grain and West Indian produce. The second part of the covering force was under the command of Rear Admiral Villaret-Joyeuse and consisted of twenty-five ships of the line, and approximately fifteen frigates and corvettes. Howe seems to have had only half as many frigates as the two French detachments—seven and three more with Montagu (one of which joined him shortly). This must have handicapped him to a degree for, if he substituted 3rd rates for frigates and they became detached for any reason, this would reduce his immediate line of battle.

The French admiral heard of the first success of this campaign, albeit unexpected, when a frigate brought him news that Nielly's squadron had captured a British frigate, the *Castor*, and a large part of a convoy from Jersey to Newfoundland. At the same time that Villaret received news of these captures, Howe learned that Montagu's squadron had recaptured some of the Newfoundland ships and gained some intelligence of Nielly's intended rendez-vous with the convoy from America. Montagu asked for reinforcements. Howe, uncertain where the French were, decided Montagu might be in danger and, given the possible routes the French might take, altered the course of the main fleet to go to his aid. Howe was still lacking hard intelligence of the where-abouts of both the convoy and the French fleet. Here his lack of frigates, a problem not unique to this action, must have played a part.[11] He does not appear to have been able to keep a close watch on either Brest or Rochefort between 5 and 18 May. He was forced to patrol with his whole fleet, but the weather had played its part in permitting the French to escape unnoticed by Howe.

On 21 May Howe's fleet sighted strange sails, which turned out to be part of the Dutch Lisbon trade that Villaret had intercepted some days previously. Howe recaptured some of the vessels, which he burnt, an expedient necessary if he was not to denude his ships of crews to man the prizes.[12] On the basis of the intelligence Howe gained from the crews of the vessels he captured, he made two decisions: one that Montagu was not in immediate danger, as he had first thought, since Villaret was to the north of him; and second, that he was going to try to intercept Villaret and the main French fleet. Howe now began a chase of the French fleet which was to culminate in the action of the Glorious First of June (see Fig. 3.iii).

On the 21 May the British fleet made some progress northward and stretched to the west; on the 22 May the wind drove them southward for which Howe has been much criticized. Between 23 and 27 May Howe came upon part of the Dutch convoy, which gave him intelligence of the whereabouts of the French fleet. On 25 May he came across a French 74 towing a brig; the 74 escaped but the brig was captured and further information was gleaned from her crew as to the movements of the French fleet. All this time Vanstabel's convoy from America was serenely sailing across the Atlantic towards the two battle fleets which were now playing cat and mouse.

Between 25 and 27 May Howe tried to manoeuvre his fleet into a position from which he could intercept Villaret's fleet. The first contact between the two fleets came on 28 May when Howe's scouting frigates signalled strange sails. The weather division of Howe's fleet was ordered to investigate and by 9 a.m. the French, for that was who it was, were bearing down on the British. There followed throughout the day a series of manoeuvres by both fleets to try to gain the advantage. Shots were exchanged between the leading ships of the British line and the French rear. This partial action continued late into the night. The British 74, the *Audacious*, was badly damaged in action with the French first rate, the *Révolutionnaire*, which, according to some accounts lost upwards of 400 men.[13] The upshot of the action was that both

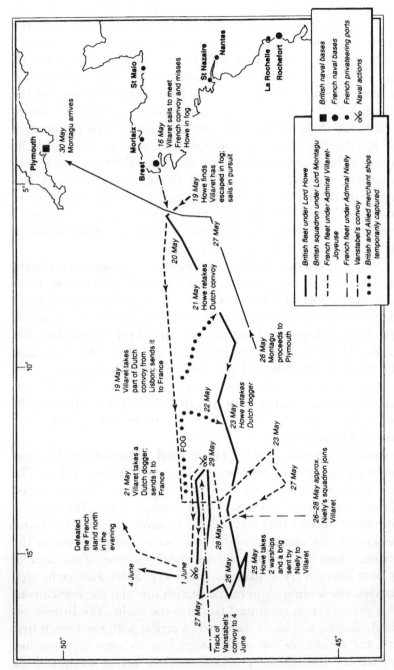

Fig. 3.iii. Chart of operations 16 May–4 June 1794.

Plymouth

30 May
Montagu arrives

Morlaix   St Malo

Brest

16 May
Villaret sails to meet
French convoy and misses
Howe in fog

St Nezaire   Nantes

La Rochelle   Rochefort

British naval bases
French naval bases
French privateering ports
Naval actions

19 May
Howe finds
Villaret has
escaped in fog;
sails in pursuit

20 May

27 May

21 May
Howe retakes
Dutch convoy

26 May
Montagu
proceeds to
Plymouth

19 May
Villaret takes
part of Dutch
convoy from
Lisbon; sends it
to France

21 May
Villaret takes a
Dutch dogger;
sends it to
France

22 May

23 May
Howe retakes
Dutch dogger

FOG

29 May

23 May

27 May

26–28 May approx.
Nielly's squadron joins
Villaret

Defeated
the French
stand north
in the
evening

1 June

27 May

26 May

28 May

25 May
Howe takes
2 warships
and a brig
sent by
Nielly to Villaret

Track of
Vanstabel's
convoy to 4
June

British fleet under Lord Howe
British squadron under Lord Montagu
French fleet under Admiral Villaret-
Joyeuse
French fleet under Admiral Nielly
Vanstabel's convoy
British and Allied merchant ships
temporarily captured

34

vessels had to return home. The *Audacious* reached Plymouth on 3 June. Howe had lost one 74-gun ship and the French one of 110 guns—an even exchange in ships but somewhat to the British advantage in force for the actions that were to follow.

Howe, terrier-like, was sticking to chasing the French fleet, whilst to the south Montagu had abandoned his search for the convoy and was returning to Plymouth. The next day, 29 May, Howe recalled his ships from the general chase which he had ordered the previous day. They were to take station in no set order but as they arrived back with the main body of the fleet. Again Howe sought to engage Villaret and ordered the leading ships of the British fleet, approaching the French on the opposite tack, to attack the French rear. There followed an attempt by Howe to gain the weather gauge of the French by passing through part of their line. This developed into another partial action with the British trying to cut off part of the French rear. The action was inconclusive in that neither gained a decisive advantage. It is obvious with hindsight that the French did not wish to be drawn into a major battle, but did wish to keep Howe occupied, and following the action Villaret sought to draw Howe to the north, away from the probable path of the approaching convoy.

Although the action of 29 May did not become general, several of the British and French vessels involved nevertheless sustained considerable damage. Particularly in the case of the British, the damage was to their masts and rigging. By 4 p.m. the action had died out with two French ships heavily damaged but covered by the rest. Eleven of the British fleet had damage to their masts and yards. Despite half the opposing fleets being engaged, casualties were relatively light, totalling no more than sixty-seven killed and 128 wounded on the British side. The damage to the masts and rigging was a greater problem. On the evening of 29 May the two fleets were approximately ten miles (sixteen kilometres) apart and once again the weather intervened. A fog came up which meant the two fleets could not keep each other in sight during the night. At approximately 9 a.m. on 30 May the fog lifted sufficiently for Howe to ascertain the motions of the French fleet. Howe tried to form a line and yet again renew the action of the preceding day. Two ships in the fleet signalled that they were not in a fit state and were given permission to quit the line. However the fog thwarted any attempt by Howe to engage the French during the 30 May.

Whilst the fog was down many of the British fleet lost station so that when it cleared on the morning of 31 May it took some time for them to regain their stations. It was not until 2 p.m. that Howe bore up on the French line. After more manoeuvring it became obvious that no action was possible before dark so Howe held off. On the evening of 28 May a part of the problem had been Howe's inability to control the British fleet in a night action against another fleet in open water (not until next morning did he discover that *Audacious* was missing). Thus it was that during the night of the 31 May Howe stationed two of his frigates to leeward to watch how the French manoeuvred in the night so that he could prepare the fleet for action against Villaret next day.

At daybreak on 1 June 1794 the British fleet stood to the westward with the wind south by west and a smooth sea. The French were now to the leeward side of the British, giving Howe the advantage for the first time of being able to decide when and where to attack. The two fleets were approximately five miles (eight kilometres) apart. At 7.16 a.m. Howe signalled that he would attack the centre of the French fleet; at 7.25 a.m. that the fleet should pass through the French line and engage to their leeward (to prevent their escape). After three days and nights of intense strain some respite was given before the action when Howe hove to and sent the crews to breakfast. At 8.12 a.m. he bore down on the French line and signalled from his flagship, the *Queen Charlotte*, for ships to engage their opposite number in the French line independently.

At 9.24 a.m. the French van opened a distant fire on the British van. At 9.52 a.m. the *Queen Charlotte* returned the fire of her French opposite number. There now evolved a series of single and multiple ship actions. These were to be bloody affairs in many cases, as many of Howe's ships sought to break through the French line and engage to leeward. However, not all of the British fleet came to close action on 1 June. Some ships came up short of the French line and cannonaded from 300–400 yards (270–360 m) to windward. But by this time Howe would have found it difficult to control the whole fleet, much of it frequently invisible in the gun-smoke. At 10.13 a.m. Howe made a signal for a general chase. By 11.30 a.m. the main part of the action was over, though firing did not cease till about 1 p.m. and it would not be until late in the afternoon that the six most heavily damaged ships would be made prize by the British or that the *Vengeur*, which had fought a series of furious actions, would sink.

Despite this, Villaret did rescue and carry away four of his most heavily damaged ships while another fought its way out of the mêlée. The British too suffered considerable damage and a high number of casualties.[14] Some 1,148 officers and men were killed and wounded in the three actions. Such was the damage to the masts and spars of the British fleet that they would lay to until 3 June to effect repairs. Howe then returned to Spithead with his prizes on 13 June, having detached nine of his line of battleships into Plymouth. The great convoy arrived at Brest without being intercepted by the British, despite the fact that Montagu had been sent out again by the Admiralty with an augmented squadron to try to intercept it. Nor was the action a total success so far as Howe was concerned. He limited the naming of meritorious officers in his despatch to five admirals, thirteen captains and two lieutenants who had taken command when their captains were wounded, and the Admiralty awarded medals only to the flag-officers and captains of sixteen ships.[15] At least one of Howe's captains, Molloy of the *Caesar*, requested and was granted a court martial into his conduct at the first of June. Although cleared of cowardice, for which he could have been executed, he was found guilty of not taking proper station and dismissed his ship. The feuds and factions still continued within the fleet.

What was the effect of the battle? In military terms Howe carried out at least some of his orders from the Admiralty. In that he had covered the outward-bound trade and watched the motions of the French fleet, and ended in engaging it, it could be argued that he had secured the Channel. What he had not been able to do was to find the convoy and, once he had gained contact with the French fleet, he seems not to have made any attempt to find where the convoy was. It could be argued that that was what Montagu had been detached for. It could also be the case that the

French fleet, by effectively trailing its coat, kept the British fleet occupied at the most vulnerable time for the convoy as it neared the French coast. By skilful manoeuvring, Villaret managed to keep out of serious trouble until 1 June. Even then he had managed to save some of his damaged ships, and most importantly of all, to get the convoy in unscathed. However, quite how important the arrival of the convoy proved to be is discussed below in Laurence Evans's article in terms which lead one to question how serious a material loss it would have been to France had it been captured. The impact on French morale would have been more than counterbalanced by the simultaneous breakout of their armies from their own frontiers to the Rhine.[16] Howe's action was in the mould of a Hawke or Vernon: to find the enemy fleet and engage it. A naval victory was more certain in its effects for Britain than the arrival of one convoy in the war at sea. It was a campaign in which Howe used all the professional tricks of his trade to bring his opponent to battle and while his victory is often described as a tactical triumph from which the French drew the immediate strategic advantage through the arrival of the convoy, there were important longer-term strategic results that also accrued to the British.

Firstly, while Villaret achieved his purpose of distracting the blockading British fleet from Vanstabel's convoy, he was unable to do so without compromising his instructions to preserve his fleet for the forthcoming invasion. The remarkable French naval build-up of 1794 was predicated on achieving a maximum fleet in size and training in the summer in order to attempt the invasion of Britain.[17] Its sortie in May was therefore premature and the loss of seven ships (the biggest French loss in battle with the Royal Navy for a hundred years) was a major setback to the invasion plans. On 12 June *The Times* triumphantly proclaimed it 'a victory, which we may say with confidence, has so crippled the navy of France, that it will be impossible for the French to send another grand fleet to sea, at least during the present campaign'.

Indeed the longer-term impact of the battle on French naval aspirations was perhaps far more damaging. It is doubtful if the French had either the material or manpower to build, equip and operate the 100 ships of the line and 127 frigates planned by the Committee of Public Safety in June 1793. The damage to the

French Mediterranean fleet during the occupation of Toulon by Britain and its allies resulted in the loss of nine of the line, about five frigates, the burning of much of the naval stores and the towing away of four of the line and seven frigates when Toulon was evacuated in the face of French counter-attack in December. All of this was a severe setback to the Committee of Public Safety's ambitious project. Nevertheless, on 10 May 1794, the Committee of Public Safety reaffirmed plans for a fleet of 100 of the line and an increased target of 160 frigates. However, the loss of a further seven ships of the line and serious damage to another five at the Glorious First of June (as well as over 7,000 seamen killed, wounded and prisoners) seems at last to have disillusioned the French government of such schemes. The shipbuilding pro-gramme slowed and France turned instead to the more successful land war on the European continent. In contrast to the first four campaign years of the American war, when France lost only four ships and could consequently expand her fleet, the French navy lost twenty-two ships in the first two years of the Revolutionary Wars and never made up these losses, while the Royal Navy continued to grow to an overwhelming supremacy.[18] The British Secretary of State for War, Henry Dundas, had the great blows against present French naval power that he sought. He now had sufficient maritime dominance to enable him to continue his campaign in the West Indies so as to prevent the future recovery of French naval power founded on the large and rich trade of those islands. He also had sufficient dominance to protect the increased British colonial commerce that provided the resources that enabled Britain to continue the war.[19]

The evidence of Lord Howe's victory was also clear enough to have an international impact. While there had been no clear result to the naval war, the neutral maritime powers had been showing signs of defending their concept of their rights as neutral traders against British search and seizure at sea, and in June 1794 a Swedish squadron joined up with a Danish squadron at Copenhagen for this purpose. However, the news of the Glorious First of June greatly boosted the British diplomatic position. The British envoy at Stockholm wrote enthusiastically that 'This decisive stroke, the effects of which will be felt in every part of Europe, has nowhere produced a deeper sensation than at this

Court . . .'. The Baltic armament became a low-key affair. The Swedes evaded American proposals for co-operation, and the American negotiator who arrived in Britain just as the news of the victory broke had to be content with a treaty which gave other advantages but said nothing about neutral rights.[20] The victory thus cleared away threats to British commerce, not just from a French naval stranglehold but also from neutral retaliation, and consequently it helped secure the economic means by which Britain could continue to fight a long war.

The British perspective for too long has sought to look at the battle in isolation. When looked at in context, some of its important features fall into place. For Britain it was vital that the French navy was defeated, the Channel secured, the revolutionary contagion kept from British shores, and that the fleet emerged in good shape. The boost to morale is not easy to measure, and may only have been temporary, followed as it was by defeats in Europe, but it was a necessary victory for giving Britain the underlying confidence to survive those continental defeats and, perhaps, for turning French ambitions elsewhere. By contributing towards deterring the French Republic from plans to build up its naval power, by removing much of the immediate French naval threat in home waters and so releasing more of the Royal Navy for the economic war overseas, and by helping deter neutrals from a more belligerent neutrality until 1801 it may have had significant long term strategic effects on the course of the war.

Notes

1. N. Hampson, *La Marine de l'an II: mobilisation de la flotte de l'Océan 1793–1794* (Paris, 1959) pp. 21–23, 72, 81–86.
2. P. Kelly, 'Strategy and Counter-Revolution: the journal of Sir Gilbert Elliot on 8–9 September 1793', *English Historical Review*, vol. 98 (1983) p. 340.
3. For the full articulation of this policy see chapter 1 of M. Duffy, *Soldiers, Sugar and Seapower. The British expeditions to the West Indies and the War against Revolutionary France* (Oxford, 1987).
4. See C. Ware, 'Toulon, 1793' in *Française et Anglais en Méditerranée* (Vincennes, Service historique de la marine, 1992) pp. 23–38.
5. For discussion of this point see chapter 8 of N. Rodger, *The*

Insatiable Earl (London, 1993). Also R.J.B. Knight, 'The Royal Navy's Recovery after the Early Phase of the American Revolutionary War' in G.J. Andreopoulos and H.E. Selesky (eds) *The Aftermath of Defeat, Armed forces and the challenge of recovery* (New Haven, 1994) pp. 12–18 and P.L.C. Webb, 'The rebuilding and repair of the fleet, 1783–93', *Bulletin of the Institute of Historical Research*, 50 (1977) pp. 194–209.

6. The second part of Rodger, *The Insatiable Earl*, discusses the whole of the naval preparations for and in the American war.

7. I owe this point to Dr Rodger's comments during discussion of this paper at the Greenwich conference on 1 June 1994.

8. PRO, ADM 2/1347, Admiralty to Howe 17 April 1794, Secret.

9. After the departure of the two India-bound ships of the line and Montagu's detachment of six, Howe's fleet comprised of the following vessels: 1st rates *Queen Charlotte, Royal George* and *Royal Sovereign*; 2nd rates *Barfleur, Impregnable, Queen, Glory*; 80-gun ships *Gibraltar, Caesar*; 74-gun 3rd rates *Bellerophon, Montagu, Tremendous, Valiant, Ramillies, Audacious, Brunswick, Alfred, Defence, Leviathan, Majestic, Invincible, Orion, Russell, Marlborough, Thunderer* and *Culloden*. In addition there were seven frigates, one hospital ship, two fireships, a sloop and two cutters.

10. Reportedly they passed close enough to hear the British fog signals of ringing bells and beating drums. W. James, *The Naval History of Great Britain* (London, 1837) vol. 1, 128.

11. A large frigate force was with the West Indies expedition, and another was guarding the Channel Islands against the invasion threat from French forces assembled at Cancale, while others engaged on the heavy routine tasks of convoy protection.

12. This was a consideration ignored both by Nielly and Villaret whose crews were consequently under-strength when the fleets finally met in battle.

13. James, *Naval History*, vol. 1, p. 132.

14. W. Laird Clowes, *The Royal Navy, A history from the earliest times to 1900* (1899, repr. London, 1997) vol. 4, p. 226.

15. Only Admiral Bowyer and not his flag-captain, Cuthbert Collingwood, of the *Barfleur* received a medal. Collingwood only received his belatedly in 1797 when he refused to accept a medal for his distinguished conduct at the battle of St Vincent until justice was done for the First of June.

16. This unfortunate outcome was not of course known to the Admiralty when it issued its orders to intercept the convoy. At that stage the allied armies in Belgium were on the offensive

themselves, and if the capture of the convoy coincided with allied victory on the frontiers it might fatally damage French morale and undermine the credibility of the Republic.

17. Prize crewmen from Nielly's squadron, captured by Montagu, boasted that they would have forty ships of the line ready in two months' time. PRO ADM 1/100 p. 325, Montagu to Howe 15 May 1794.

18. Hampson, *La Marine de l'an II*, pp. 72, 90, 214; J. R. Dull, 'Why did the French Revolutionary Navy fail?' in *Proceedings of the Consortium on Revolutionary Europe* (1989) vol. 2, pp. 121–37, particularly p. 127.

19. See Duffy, *Soldiers, Sugar and Seapower*, *passim*, particularly chapter 15.

20. British Library, Add Mss 34,470, Lord Hugh Spencer to Lord Grenville 4 July 1794; S.F. Bemis, *Jay's Treaty. A Study of Commerce and Diplomacy* (New Haven, 1962) pp. 299–373.

DOCUMENT 3.*i*

THE ADMIRALTY'S INSTRUCTIONS TO EARL HOWE, 17 APRIL 1794

(Source: PRO ADM 1/1347—Secret Letters [Office Copy])

Secret   By etc.

As soon as the several ships of the Fleet under your Lordship's command, lately returned from their cruize, are in all respects refitted, You are to put to sea the first opportunity of wind & weather, and proceed off of Ushant, giving protection, on their passage down Channel, to such outward bound Convoys as may be at Spithead ready to sail, but more particularly to the East India Convoy, under the charge of His Majesty's ship Suffolk. And your Lordship is further directed, after having proceeded off Ushant, to detach one of the Rear Admirals of the Fleet under your command, with such a Force as, according to the best intelligence you may be able to procure, you may judge to be necessary for the sake of giving protection to the East India Convoy on their passage across the Bay; directing the said Rear Admiral, after having seen them in safety as far as your Lordship shall think expedient, to join you, at such Rendezvous, and at such time, as you shall appoint.

And Whereas Intelligence has been received that a very large and valuable Fleet of Merchant ships may be shortly expected from America under convoy of a French Squadron (Copies of which Intelligence are herewith inclosed), And Whereas the attempting to intercept the same is an object of the most urgent importance to the success of the present war, your Lordship is hereby required and directed to give orders to the Rear Admiral (to be detached to a certain distance with the East India Convoy as aforesaid) after performing that service to cruize, for such time as you think proper, from Cape Ortegal to the Latitude of Belle Isle, for the sake of intercepting the same accordingly. Or you will make a detachment of any other part of the Fleet under your command for the performance of this service, as to your Lordship may appear most adviseable.

Your Lordship is further instructed to make such a general disposition of the Fleet under your command, and to take such a Station or

Stations, & for such time as you shall judge most proper, for the sake of protecting the Trade of His Majesty's subjects & of His Allies coming into and going out of the Channel, as well as of intercepting, and taking or destroying, the ships of War, Privateers and Trade of the Enemy bearing always in mind that a due regard to the Security of the Kingdoms of Great Britain and Ireland must ever form one of the most essential and constant Objects of your care & attention.

Your Lordship will consider yourself at liberty to send into Port, from time to time, such of the Ships of your Fleet as you may think proper for the sake of refreshment, giving their Captains orders to join you again or otherwise as you shall judge best for His Majesty's Service. You will also be at liberty to send Detachments from you whenever you judge it necessary to cruize on separate Stations for the better meeting with Ships of the Enemy and to give them such Orders as you may think proper for that purpose. And whenever you may return to Port, you will leave sufficient Cruizers for the purpose of watching the motions of the Enemy and of protecting the Trade of His Majesty's subjects.

And Whereas Rear Admiral Macbride has been appointed to the command of a separate Squadron for the purpose of attending more immediately to the safety of the Islands of Guernsey & Jersey, and of watching the Armaments reported to be carrying on in the Ports of the Opposite Coast from Dieppe as far westward as the Isle of Bas; and Whereas the said Rear Admiral is instructed to keep up a constant communication with your Lordship, and to co-operate with the Fleet under your command for the protection of the coast and the security of the Trade of His Majesty's Subjects in the channel, and also to follow such directions as he may receive from your Lordship (not inconsistent with the general object of his Instructions), Your Lordship is hereby required and directed to communicate with the said Rear Admiral accordingly; to furnish him with copies of your Rendezvous & Private Signals; and to give him such directions for his conduct, from time to time, as you shall judge most conducive to the good of His Majesty's service, sending Copies thereof to our secretary for our Information.

Your Lordship will also transmit to our Secretary, before you sail, a copy of your intended Rendezvous & of the signals by which the ships & vessels of the Fleet under your command may be known; and you will send him, during your cruize, frequent accounts of your proceedings and of any intelligence you may procure that may be necessary to be communicated to us. Your Lordship will continue your cruize so long as you shall judge adviseable according to circumstances and the Intelligence you may obtain of the proceedings of the enemy; returning to Torbay (or Spithead) whenever you judge it expedient, and holding your Fleet in constant readiness to proceed to sea whenever the Objects pointed out in these Instructions, and the good of His Majesty's service, may render it necessary.

Given etc. 17 April 1794
Chatham
Arden
P. Affleck

To
The Earl Howe Admiral & Commander
in Chief of His Majesty's Fleet employed
& to be employed in the Channel Soundings or
wherever else His Majesty's service may require

4

The Glorious First of June
The British View of the Actions of 28, 29 May and 1 June 1794

Roger Morriss

The encounter between the British and French fleets between 28 May and 1 June 1794 was precipitated by the mutual interest of both Admiral Richard, Earl Howe and Rear Admiral Louis-Thomas Villaret-Joyeuse in the French convoy carrying food supplies from the Chesapeake under Rear Admiral Pierre Jean Vanstabel. While Howe intended its capture or destruction, Villaret had to provide for its safe conduct into port. The different motives of the protagonists permitted their separate advocates different interpretations of the outcome of their encounter. The political situation in each fleet, and in France and Britain, helped to give each of these explanations different emphases.[1] Difficulties in deciding precisely what happened have consequently been understandable. It is the object here to provide an outline of events illustrated by a series of personal accounts written by participants that together reveal how the British viewed the battle.

The accounts of participants

A great many British accounts of the battle survive. All the commissioned officers, as well as the ships' masters, had to keep official logs; some also kept private journals; and representative specimens for each ship have been printed in *Logs of the Great Sea Fights, 1794–1805*, published by the Navy Records Society in 1899. Twenty-eight of the British ships that took part in the battle are represented in this volume. Being, for the most part, official records, these accounts are limited to the manoeuvres of ships. They include the signals, with their numbers, which were available to Lord Howe between 28 May and 1 June 1794, and were cited in many of the official records. The availability of the officers' point of view has also been enhanced by the publication of letters and reminiscences that cover the battle: for example, those of Sir William Dillon and Sir Edward Codrington.[2] Inevitably, however, officers' accounts are limited by the purposes for which the authors wrote: formal logs omit personal experience, anecdote and gossip, and are limited to the official proceedings of ships, while many reports and letters to superiors tend to be self-justificatory. Above all, officers' accounts tend to overlook what was going on among the seamen within their ships.

The objective here has been to enlarge this view of the battle, and to represent the variety of differing social viewpoints possessed by commentators in the British fleet. The officers' view remains, but here also are the views of an artist, a seaman and a very young midshipman. All have a particular value in emanating from ships that took major parts or occupied key situations in the battle. At the same time, some of the writers occupied positions within their ships that permitted them to observe what was going on among the seamen, and their relationships with officers. None of these accounts are well known: they have either not been published before or had a limited circulation. Together, they provide a perspective that is more rounded than hitherto available. Above all, though not selected for this reason, they reveal why those who fought in the battle realized that they had participated in one of the great events in the history of British warfare.

Of these accounts, that which has the widest perspective was produced by the artist Nicholas Pocock to accompany four bird's-eye views of the battle (see Document 4.i on page 73). He was stationed on a signal-repeating frigate, the *Pegasus* lying off the

British line near to the *Queen Charlotte*, Howe's flagship. In addition to providing a succinct summary of the British admiral's main signals, Pocock was trying to visualize and represent what was going on over the whole changing vista of battle. His commentary, supplementing four sketches, thus provides an overview that no single other written account can rival. It is written, moreover, by a person who was relatively independent of service politics. He reported actually what he saw, without introducing hearsay, interpretations or official jargon to which naval personnel were liable. For Pocock, ignorance of precisely what was happening was no shame: 'ships dismasted' could 'emerge from the smoke in such a manner that we could not see even who they had engaged last'. Indeed, Pocock's accuracy is, if anything, his greatest weakness; for where he could not see, his account loses coherence, to improve again when visibility improved.

How Pocock came to be in the *Pegasus* is uncertain. Was he appointed to act the role of official war artist?[3] His biographer is silent on the subject. Nevertheless as a self-employed artist, it may be presumed he arranged the voyage either through the Admiralty, with Lord Howe, or directly with Captain Robert Barlow. At the time he was collaborating with Joseph Farrington to produce a series of bird's-eye views of the royal dockyards for the Navy Board, so he may have been at Portsmouth when Howe's fleet set sail.[4] Yet his activity was not confined to his bird's-eye views. He seems to have been able to benefit financially from his voyage by producing oil paintings such as that representing the action of the *Brunswick* with the *Vengeur*, presumably for which purpose he also produced sketches of parts of the battle as from water-level, some of which, with his bird's-eye views, are in the National Maritime Museum.

At the other extreme from Pocock's panorama is the lower-deck letter of Jonathan Wilkinson, a seaman on the *Queen*, the 98 gun flagship of Rear Admiral Alan Gardner (see Document 4.ii on page 80). More exactly, as Wilkinson proclaims, although he served at a gun during the actions, at other times he acted as a steward in the officers' wardroom. Wilkinson in June 1794 was twenty-eight years old and had served on board the *Queen* since January 1793.[5] In his earlier life he had been employed on the farm of John Clark, tenant farmer to the Duke of Portland in the neighbourhood of Kirkby-in-Ashfield, Nottinghamshire, and it is to him that Wilkinson proudly writes. Though from a humble background, Wilkinson felt distinguished by having been with the fleet that had returned to Portsmouth with six prizes and been honoured with a ceremonial visit by George III and Queen Charlotte. He was clearly conscious of having taken part in events that had made history, and it was this sense of the remarkable that he wished to convey to all his friends and acquaintances at home. To his former employer, with whom he hoped to regain employment one day, he clearly assumed his experience had given him added value as a potential employee.

From his low profile, Wilkinson is unable to include in his account all that happened: he omits, for example, the engagement of 28 May, presumably because the *Queen*, though firing shot at a distance, never came into action, and because that evening, when the main action occurred, Wilkinson was probably busy attending to the officers and remained ignorant of such matters as the presumed surrender of the *Révolutionnaire*. Though lacking knowledge of events beyond his ship, and despite his colloquial literacy, Wilkinson reveals the environment below decks like no other writer connected with this battle. Wilkinson had entered the navy in 1791 and this was clearly his first experience of the devastation of battle. So close was the action—on 1 June the *Queen* barely cleared her opponent—that the port at which his gun fired had four shot enter, to kill two men and wound five. Wilkinson himself was wounded and he wrote only after recovering from his wounds. Yet, with the experience still vivid in his mind, he provided a remarkably illuminating insight into the conditions seamen endured. With the other gun crews, he lay on the decks at the guns for two nights and three days. As he suggests, the tension of those men below decks was virtually palpable, and justifiably so. For when battle came, as he says, it was as though the very elements were on fire, the shot flying about the ship like a hailstorm.

The letter of William Parker to his father is comparable in its attempts to convey the effect of shot and responses of seamen in the heat of battle (see Document 4.iii on page 83). A new midshipman only thirteen years old, Parker was the nephew of Sir John Jervis, later Earl St Vincent, and had entered the navy in

1793 as a captain's servant to John Duckworth, commanding the *Orion* in 1794. For pay purposes, Parker was made up to midshipman in April 1794 though not, according to his letter, to the knowledge of Duckworth. During the battle, he was stationed in the captain's cabin which would have been cleared for action as part of the gun deck. There, at one stage on 1 June, a red hot shot from the enemy kept rolling about and burning everybody until Roger Mears, the *Orion's* first lieutenant, 'took it up in his speaking trumpet & threw it overboard'.

Though stationed below during action, Parker had the freedom to wander on deck and observe the eagerness of the seamen for battle, and the manner in which Duckworth managed his crew during the difficult time before engagement commenced. He conveys with unusual poignancy the intimacy of the relationship between captain and crew. At one stage on 29 May Duckworth hauled cheering seamen out of the rigging by their legs; at another on the 1 June he denies appeals to fire until the *Orion* was appropriately positioned, when in his turn he appealed to his men to 'Fire my boys. Fire.' The closeness of the relationship, strengthened through the chaos and devastation of battle, encompassed deep understanding and compassion: the drunkenness, mutiny, contrition and pardoning of the crew that followed the return to port reveals much about the nature of the British navy at the beginning the French Revolutionary War. Parker, though only a boy, had already been initiated into the intimacies of the navy, partly by an experienced seaman who had taught him seamanship and had been killed in the action of 1 June. His concern for that man's wife and children reflected the paternalism that was both part of society on shore and the unseen cement of the British navy.

As an officer in training, Parker appears to have mixed freely with the officers of the *Orion* and kept a journal, from which he was able to write a full account of what was happening beyond as well as within the ship. Unlike other officers, however, Parker picked up the gossip going about between decks, some of which arose in communication between ships, even between the British and French, and conveys the nicknaming, the threats, the scorn and rivalry that passed across the dividing water. As he reveals, a relationship developed between enemies, surprisingly not purely based on animosity; after the stress of battle, on the sinking of the *Vengeur*, British seamen wept for the hundreds of French men drowned before their eyes.

Perhaps naturally, the pathos of battle is missing from the letter of Rowland Bevan who was second lieutenant of the *Brunswick* that engaged the *Vengeur* and was primarily responsible for reducing the latter to a sinking state (see Document 4.iv on page 93). Bevan, a lieutenant since 1790, in his letter to T. Morgan of Swansea, is principally concerned with manoeuvres. Yet, in her three-hour duel with the *Vengeur*, during which at one stage she also engaged the *Achille*, the *Brunswick* suffered the heaviest casualties of all the British ships—forty-four killed and 113 wounded—and Bevan was one of the wounded. At the time of writing, Bevan was still unsure whether he would lose a leg, and his recuperative state perhaps explains the limitations of his letter, for he mentions the *Vengeur* duel only in passing and omits reference to the *Achille* altogether.

Bevan's letter to Morgan is complemented by an account of the battle attributed to Bevan which seems to have been intended, with another by William Kemble, third lieutenant of the *Brunswick*, for use by Nicholas Pocock in painting two pictures of the duel. Both these accounts were printed by the Navy Records Society in 1928.[6] The style of the latter account is very different from that of the letter to Morgan, printed here, and it includes far more detail of the entanglement with the *Vengeur* and the gunnery methods adopted by the British ship. The author was stationed on a gun deck and was fully aware of the threat and exertions demanded by the approach of the *Achille*. Again, Bevan provides some anecdotes of particular actions by seaman, but his main heroes are his captain, John Harvey, wounded three times and eventually to die after an arm amputation, and his brother, Captain Henry Harvey of the *Ramillies* which, to the elation of the seamen, came to the rescue of the *Brunswick* when she was engaged on two sides by *Vengeur* and *Achille*.[7] In this account Bevan explains his lack of compassion for the French by the suffering inflicted by the French on the crew of the *Brunswick*: after the *Vengeur* had struck her colours, and despite her appeals for help, 'we could not lend them assistance, nor after the villainous manner they fired did any of them deserve quarter.

Their langridge was raw ore and their sulphur pots scalded our people so very miserably that they wished for death to end their agony.'[8]

The account of Captain Berkeley, finished by Jonathan Monkton, his first lieutenant in the *Marlborough*, has similarities with those of Bevan (see Document 4.v on page 96).[9] Berkeley writes to Lord Howe, at the latter's request, to report his ship's proceedings and observations during the three days of action. Mindful of his 'Lordship's intention', his report echoes the signals *Marlborough* received and her engagements with *Impétueux* and *Mucius*. *Marlborough* was severely damaged and received casualties —twenty-nine killed and ninety wounded—in total second only to the *Brunswick*. Berkeley too was wounded. His first lieutenant took command and therefore completed the report. Dismasted, Monckton's immediate problem was not the fire of the enemy, the *Impétueux* having virtually ceased fighting, but the 'friendly fire' of British ships, which mistook the St George's ensign on the stump of the foremast for the tricolour flag of the French. Like the other contemporary accounts that follow, however, the principal message Berkeley conveyed was the discipline and accuracy of the *Marlborough*'s gunfire and the 'coolness, obedience and bravery' of her seamen. It was message that was representative of almost all the British ships.

The engagement of 28 May[10]

These five accounts by British participants need to be placed in their context. Although the main battle took place on 1 June 1794, the preliminary skirmishing began four days earlier. The reconnoitring frigates of the British fleet first sighted the French fleet at 6.30 a.m. on 28 May 1794 in latitude (at noon) 47 degrees 34 minutes north, longitude 13 degrees 39 minutes west of Greenwich—about 429 miles (686 kilometres) west of Ushant. They immediately signalled sighting strange sails south south-east. There were twenty-six French ships of the line besides frigates. Howe too had twenty-six of the line.

The British fleet had the wind from south by west on the starboard bow and Howe ordered Rear Admiral Pasley, commanding a flying column of four ships of the line on his

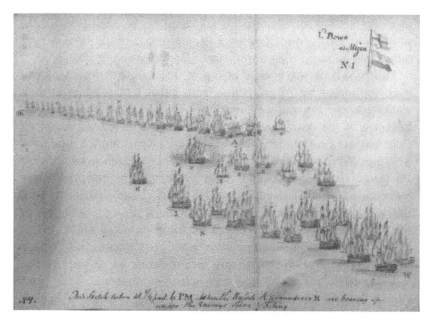

Fig. 4.i.   Nicholas Pocock's 'Sketch No. 1: The engagement of 28 May'.

Artist's notes: 'This sketch was taken at ¼ past 6 PM. When *Russell* A & *Thunderer* B are bearing up under the Enemy's Stern & Firing. A. *Russell* firing on the Enemy's rear ship; B. *Thunderer*, firing but farther astern; C. *Bellerophon*, firing on the Enemy's Quarter; D. *Marlborough* having fired and dropped into the Rear; E. *Leviathan* coming up with all Sail set; F. *Audacious* coming up also—; G. *Gibraltar* coming up under Crowded Sail; H. The *Caesar* gaining ahead of the *Queen Charlotte*; I. *Queen Charlotte*; K. The Remainder of our fleet in chase, and without any prescribed order; A. *Pegasus*; B. *Niger*; C. *Latona*; No 1. The Sternmost Ship of the Enemy's line a 3 deck; 26. Their van Ship.'

weather bow, to reconnoitre. By 9 a.m. the French fleet, having wore, was heading towards the British fleet, which cleared for action. An hour later the French fleet was still ten miles (sixteen kilometres) distant, formed in a rough line ahead on the port tack, when it hauled to the wind for ships to change sails and to facilitate communication. The British fleet, still maintaining two columns, just after 10.30 a.m. wore round in succession on to the same tack as the French which, at 1 p.m. again made sail and tacked, upon which Pasley's squadron was ordered to harass their rear. At 1.45 p.m. the French appeared to be taking avoiding action and Howe signalled for a general chase; by 2.30 p.m. the range was no more than a mile and first shots were exchanged.

Full broadside fire opened at 6 p.m. Pasley's squadron took the lead, supported by 74-gun ships from Howe's main force as they could get up. Pocock well describes the scene, as does Captain Berkeley of the *Marlborough* in his letter to Lord Howe.[11] Attention was concentrated on the rear ship of the French line, the 110-gun *Révolutionnaire*, which first lost her mizzen mast and, by 10 p.m., also her fore and main yards and maintopsail yard. Surrounded by British ships, and having ceased returning fire, she was deemed to have struck her colours. Indeed Berkeley in the *Marlborough* believed she had struck and was taken prize. However, these were assumptions made as darkness fell, which the limitations of night signals did nothing to dispel. In the morning *Révolutionnaire* was still adrift, a mastless hulk, and French frigates were hastening to her assistance. Her last British opponent, the also damaged *Audacious*, was deterred from getting at her and *Révolutionnaire* was eventually taken in tow and brought safely into Rochefort. The captain of the British 74 *Audacious* also decided his ship was so badly damaged that she had to return for dockyard repair. The engagement of 28 May consequently reduced the opposing fleets each by one ship.

The engagement of 29 May

At daybreak, with the wind from south-by-west, the fleets were approximately six miles apart, with the French having the wind on the weather bow of the British, both being on the starboard tack. At 7.30 a.m., with the intention of attacking the French rear, Lord Howe ordered the British to tack in succession. Now with the wind to port, Howe subsequently ordered his fleet to pass through the French line in order to obtain the weather gauge. However, at 8 a.m. Villaret ordered his van to wear in succession to support his rear. They accordingly began to run down the leeward side of their line and where they hauled close to the wind, in order to keep their advantage, on a port tack parallel to the British fleet. In this manoeuvring, as the British van approached the French rear, the latter opened a distant fire, which

Fig. 4.ii. Nicholas Pocock's 'Sketch No. 2: The engagement of 29 May'.

Artist's notes: 'This Sketch taken at ½ past 11 when Ld. Howe made the
Signal to Tack in succession from the Van. A. *Caesar* not being able
to comply with Signal to Tack; B. *Queen*; C. *Russell*; D. *Valiant*;
E. *Royal George*; F. *Invincible*; G. *Orion*; H. *Majestic*; I. *Leviathan*; K. *Queen
Charlotte*; L. *Bellerophon*; M. *Marlborough*; N. *Royal Sovereign*; O. *Ramillies*;
P. *Tremendous*; Q. *Montagu*; R. *Alfred*; S. *Brunswick*; T. *Culloden*;
U. *Gibraltar*; V. *Barfleur*; W. *Glory*; X. *Impregnable*; Y. *Thunderer*;
Z. *Defence*.'

was returned as the British ships came up and passed. The vans of
the two fleets then came on to parallel tacks and closed; fire was
exchanged and some damage done on both sides.

At 11.30 a.m., as Pocock observed, Howe again signalled for
his fleet to tack in succession and attempted to gain the weather
gauge but, the British fleet being insufficiently advanced to cut
off more than a few ships in the French rear, the order was
annulled. An hour later, Howe repeated the signal to tack. This
time it remained unseen, obscured by smoke, was only partially
obeyed, and was again annulled. It was repeated at 1.15 p.m. and
though the leading British ship, the *Caesar*, was unable to obey

through damage, several others engaged the rear of the French line. Impatient now that his orders were not being fully obeyed for a variety of reasons, Howe in the *Queen Charlotte* tacked, though not his turn in the succession, hauled east-south-east and effected a break through the French line between the sixth and seventh ships from the French rear. She was followed by the *Bellerophon* and *Leviathan*, the remainder of the British vessels passing to the rear of the French line.

Though the British fleet had now gained the weather gauge, several British ships had been damaged in the operation. In his letter to his father on 17 June 1794, William Parker—with the fresh eye of a youth—observed how the French attempted to disable their enemies by firing at their rigging.[12] Parker's ship, the *Orion*, was damaged in this way. Several British ships were forced to lie-to, preventing them from obeying a signal from Howe to tack and engage in a chase that would undoubtedly have resulted in a general mêlée. Anyway, at this time Villaret was taking measures to rescue two vessels at the rear of the French line, the *Tyrannicide*, 74, and *Indomptable*, 80, which lay disabled and surrounded by British ships. To save these vessels, Villaret vainly made the signal for his fleet to wear, then wore himself in the *Montagne*, turning on the starboard tack at the head of his own line. His former leading ship, the *Montagnard*, 74, failed to turn and continued upon the port tack; damaged, she kept her course until she was taken in tow by a frigate, eventually to be found by Vanstabel and taken into his convoy. Meanwhile, in a manoeuvre which was much praised by Pocock in the *Pegasus*, the French fleet ran down, extracted *Tyrannicide* and *Indomptable*, when Villaret again wore and stood away on the port tack. In the process, he conceded the weather gauge. Howe, meanwhile, could only reform his line as most convenient and keep in contact with the French as night fell.

The events of 30 and 31 May

That night the two fleets maintained their formations about ten miles (sixteen kilometres) apart, the French bearing north-west on the British lee bow. The wind had come round to the south-west, and the weather thickened. Next morning, 30 May, when the weather cleared, the French were still north-west of the British fleet but on the starboard tack until Villaret put them about to port. For his part, Howe reformed and at 10 a.m. directed his fleet to form two columns. However, the fog returned and the two fleets lost sight of one another, when Howe directed his ships to come to the wind on the port tack in succession. Even so, few ships could see their closest neighbours and the British fleet gradually became much scattered in consequence.

At 9 a.m. on 31 May the weather again cleared and the two fleets resighted one another. The French were to the north of the British and consisted of thirty-two ships, including twenty-six of the line. Observers in the British fleet—the young William Parker among them—were surprised to note that nearly all the French ships looked in good condition. It was afterwards discovered that Villaret had been joined on 30 May by Rear Admiral Nielly with three ships of the line. Though the crippled *Tyrannicide* remained with the fleet, Villaret had taken advantage of this reinforcement to send the crippled *Indomptable* back to port under tow of a frigate.[13]

About 2 p.m. Howe began to manoeuvre his line towards the French who, however, edged away, forming their line on the port tack. At 3.30 p.m. Howe reformed his line and continued to move towards the French. At 5 p.m. the fleets were five miles (eight kilometres) apart and Howe made signals for his van, centre and rear to attack their opposites in the enemy line. By 7 p.m., however, mindful perhaps of the confusion that arose on 28 May when, by default, the *Révolutionnaire* was permitted to escape, Howe seems to have decided that difficulties of communication after dark made a daylight engagement preferable. Annulling his previous directions, he ordered his fleet to stand closer to the wind on the port tack.[14] That night, to prevent any possibility of Villaret attempting to seize the weather gauge, communication frigates were stationed about a mile to the lee of the British fleet to keep watch on the French. In this pattern, the two fleets continued on westward parallel courses throughout the night of 31 May.

The battle of 1 June: The main manoeuvres

At first light on 1 June, in latitude 47 degrees 48 minutes North, longitude 18 degrees 30 minutes West, the French fleet was six miles (about ten kilometres) north of the British, on its starboard or lee bow and still steering in line of battle on the port tack. The wind was a moderate breeze from south-by-west and the sea was calm. At 5 a.m. Howe signalled for the British to steer north-west and at 6 a.m., to steer north. At 7.16, when the two fleets were three to four miles (five to six kilometres) apart, he signalled that he would attack the French centre, and at 7.25 a.m. that he would break through their line and engage from leeward. This was nevertheless qualified for captains unable to follow their Admiral's example by the signal at 8.30 a.m. for each ship independently to steer for and engage her opponent in the enemy line.[15]

About 7.30 a.m., though preparing to engage, Howe hove-to and ordered his crews go to breakfast. At 8.12 a.m. the British resumed steering towards the French, when Howe signalled for each ship to make for and engage her opposite number in the French line. At this, the *Royal Sovereign, Royal George* and *Barfleur*, all of ninety-eight or a hundred guns, changed places with ships of lesser rate[16] in order to match enemy units of similar force.

The British fleet was then formed in line abreast, from its van to its rear as follows[17]:

Caesar, 80, Captain A.J.P. Molloy;
Bellerophon, 74, Captain W.J. Hope, Rear Admiral T. Pasley;
Leviathan, 74, Lord Hugh Seymour;
Russell, 74, Captain J.W. Payne;
Royal Sovereign, 100, Captain H. Nicholls, Admiral Thomas Graves;
Marlborough, 74, Captain G.C. Berkeley;
Defence, 74, Captain J. Gambier;
Impregnable, 98, Captain G.B. Westcott, Rear Admiral B. Caldwell;
Tremendous, 74, Captain J. Pigot;
Barfleur, 98, Captain C. Collingwood, Rear Admiral G. Bowyer;
Invincible, 74, Captain T. Pakenham;

Culloden, 74, Captain I. Schomberg;
Gibraltar, 80, Captain T. Mackenzie;
Queen Charlotte, 100, Captain R. Curtis, Admiral Earl Howe;
Brunswick, 74, Captain John Harvey;
Valiant, 74, Captain T. Pringle;
Orion, 74, Captain J.T. Duckworth;
Queen, 98, Captain J. Hutt, Rear Admiral A. Gardner;
Ramillies, 74, Captain Henry Harvey;
Alfred, 74, Captain John Bazely;
Montagu, 74, Captain James Montagu;
Royal George, 100, Captain William Domett, Admiral Sir
   Alexander Hood;
Majestic, 74, Captain C. Cotton;
Glory, 98, Captain J. Elphinstone;
Thunderer, 74, Captain A. Bertie.

The French fleet, formed in a close head to stern line, bore east to west. There is considerable disagreement between sources regarding both the ships that were present and their precise order in the French line.[18] The most recent work confirms the following ships were present; their order, beginning at the van or west end, was probably close to that which follows.[19]

Le Trajan, 74, Captain Dumoutier;
L'Eole, 74, Captain Bertrand Keranguen;
L'America, 74, Captain Louis L'Heritier;
Le Téméraire, 74, Captain Morel;
Le Terrible, 110, Captain J. Le Ray, Rear Admiral
   François-Joseph Bouvet;
L'Impétueux, 74, Captain Douville;
Le Mucius, 74, Captain Larregny;
Le Tourville, 74, Captain Langlois;
Le Gasparin, 74, Captain Tardy;
Le Convention, 74, Captain Joseph Allary;
Le Trente-et-un Mai, 74, Captain Honoré Ganteaume;
Le Tyrannicide, 74, Captain Dordelin;
Le Juste, 80, Captain Blavet;
Le Montagne, 120, Captain Bazire, Rear Admiral Louis-Thomas
   Villaret-Joyeuse;
Le Jacobin, 80, Captain Gassin;
L' Achille, 74, Captain La Villegris;

Le Vengeur du Peuple, 74, Captain Jean-François Renaudin;
La Patriote, 74, Captain Lucadou;
Le Northumberland, 74, Captain François Etienne;
L'Entreprenant, 74, Captain Lefrancq;
Le Jemappes, 80, Captain Desmartis;
Le Neptune, 74, Captain Tiphaine;
Le Pelletier, 74, Captain Berade;
Le Républicain, 110, Captain Longer, Rear Admiral
   Joseph-Marie Nielly;
Le Sans-Pareil, 80, Captain Jean-François Courand;
Le Scipion, 80, Captain Huguet.

Under single-reefed topsails, the two fleets approached one another, sailing at little more than five knots. As their lines became irregular, some ships lay to, while others backed and filled to keep their stations and distances. About 9.24 a.m. the French began to fire upon the British van as its closest ship, the *Defence*, came into range. Firing then became general.

At the head of the British line, events were not propitious. As on 29 May, the line was led by the fast sailing *Caesar*, captained by Anthony Molloy, a friend of Sir Roger Curtis, Howe's flag captain; but soon after the French began firing, the *Caesar* dropped astern and brought-to over 500 yards (450 metres) to windward of the enemy. Molloy later maintained that he had never intended to break though the French line for, as the leading ship in the British line, his opposite French number, the *Trajan*, would have been able to shoot ahead if he had attempted to attack her from her stern or by passing behind her to leeward. He thus intended to attack from her weather quarter but, as he tried to take that position, a shot drove 'a splinter and three parts of the fore-tackle fall into the starboard quarter-block of the tiller-rope'. The latter became jammed in the sheave, preventing the rudder from moving and this remained undiscovered for half an hour.

Elsewhere, however, events were taking a decisive turn. Flying the signal for close action, at 9.30 a.m. the *Queen Charlotte* was steering a slanting course for the stern of the *Montagne*. At that time she was receiving the fire of the *Vengeur*, third in line behind the French flagship and already engaged by the *Brunswick*.

Ignoring the *Vengeur*, Howe set sail and came up with the *Achille*, whose fire he returned, but only from his upper and middle decks, ordering the guns on his first and second decks to reserve their fire for the *Montagne* upon whose port quarter he was approaching. Steering so close under the French flagship's stern that her flagstaff brushed the *Queen Charlotte*'s main and mizen shrouds, Howe fired her full broadside into the French stern, then bore hard to port, close up against the starboard side of the *Montagne*. Sheltering on that side of the French flagship was the *Jacobin*, almost becalmed, the wind taken from her sails and the *Queen Charlotte* engaged her to starboard as well as the *Montagne*, now to port. A shot from the *Jacobin*, however, cut away the *Queen Charlotte*'s foretopmast, temporarily handicapping her from further engagement with Villaret, who at 10.10 a.m. set more sail and ranged ahead of Howe (see Fig. 4.iii). The stern-frame and starboard quarter of the *Montagne* were badly shattered and she had suffered around 300 casualties. Villaret thus deliberately removed the *Montagne* clear of further fire while the *Jacobin* also steered clear, leaving the *Queen Charlotte* to engage the *Juste*.

Thinking from these manoeuvres that the French might intend to avoid a full fleet engagement, Howe signalled for a general chase. Following Howe's example, five British ships in addition to the *Queen Charlotte* broke through the French line and engaged their opponents from leeward.[20] The remainder hauled up and opened fire from windward, some at long range, others more closely. Thereafter the battle broke into clusters, individual ships manoeuvring to gain the advantage of immediate antagonists, the damage inflicted by either side invariably resulting from the capacity of British or French ships to support one another against single opponents. In these duels, the French were not always worsted. *Bellerophon*, though attempting to engage the *Eole* suffered badly from two passing French ships and had to call the frigate *Latona* to her assistance. The *Leviathan*, while engaging the *America*, was subject to attack in passing from *Eole* and *Trajan*. The latter ships also attacked the *Russell* after that ship was damaged in action with her opposite number, the *Téméraire*. Similarly, after engaging the *Terrible*, the *Royal Sovereign* was attacked by *Montagne* and *Jacobin*.

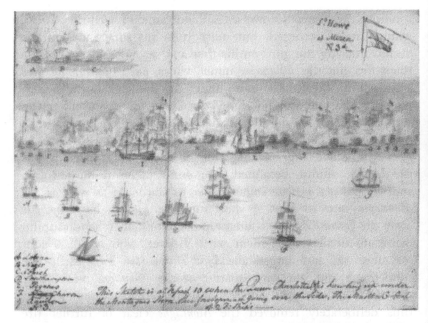

Fig. 4.iii. Nicholas Pocock's 'Sketch No. 3: 'The battle of 1 June'.

Artist's notes: 'This Sketch is at ½ past 10 when the *Queen Charlotte* (K) is hawling up under the *Montagne's* Stern. Her foretopmast going over the Side. The *Marlbro* G foul of 2 F{rench} ships—A. *Caesar* Van Ship of Our fleet Engaging their Van; B. *Bellerophon*; C. *Leviathan*; D. *Royal Sovereign* driving & chasing a 3 decker out of the line; E. *Barfleur*; F. *Impregnable*; G. *Marlborough*; H. *Defence*; I. *Invincible*; J. *Tremendous* M Stays & Rigging Cut to pieces; K. *Queen Charlotte* luffing up under *Montagne's* Stern; L. *Gibraltar*; M. *Brunswick* on board a French ship (*Vengeur*); N. *Queen*; O. *Orion*; P. *Royal George*; Q. *Montagu*; R. *Glory*; S. *Thunderer*; A. *Latona*; B. *Niger*; C. *Comet*; D. *Southampton*; E. *Pegasus*; F. *Charon*; G. *Aquilon.*'

Marlborough was put in particular peril by such combined forces. Captain Berkeley's letter reveals the extent to which she was reduced to a wreck, her opponent, the *Impétueux*, having become entangled in her shrouds, to be joined by the *Mucius*, which fell across the bow of the *Marlborough*. The three ships formed a triangle, the masts of all three being shot away. From her state and inactivity, the *Impétueux* was thought to have surrendered, but before the *Marlborough* could extract herself, she was attacked by the *Montagne*. The British ship suffered twenty-nine killed and ninety wounded.

Much of this engagement over a broad area was covered by gun smoke. The degree of obscurity may be judged from Pocock's sketch of the situation at 10.30 in the morning of 1 June (see Fig. 4.iii). The same sketch reveals the location of frigates employed on both sides to repeat the signals of the flagships: on the British side, the *Pegasus* for the *Queen Charlotte*, the *Niger* for the *Royal Sovereign* and the *Aquilon* for the *Royal George*. The French possessed more frigates for this purpose and the manoeuvres of the French admiral indicate that he made full use of them, as far as he was able, to keep his fleet in line and provide crippled ships with support.

As though to avoid the mêlée that was developing, at about 10.10 a.m. Villaret in the *Montagne* made sail ahead, followed by his second astern and such others of the French line that had not suffered significant mast and rigging damage, until they were nearly abreast of the French van. There, the flagship wore round and, with eleven sail in her wake, stood towards the British first rate, *Queen*, then lying crippled. Howe in *Queen Charlotte*, with the assistance of five other vessels rallied by signal, made sail to reach the *Queen*. This manoeuvre deterred Villaret, who simply fired on the *Queen* from a distance. By then, further east, five other French ships had been crippled, two dismasted, and were being taken in tow. Villaret consequently maintained sail with consorts in company, to provide these vessels with support.

The *Brunswick* and the *Vengeur*

In these manoeuvres, written from the British viewpoint, it is easy to assume that engagements were perfunctory, and that the French were easy victims. Nothing does more to dispel this impression than the engagement between the *Brunswick* and the *Vengeur*.

The *Brunswick* was perhaps the most damaged vessel on the British side. In attempting to press through the French line, at 9.45 a.m. she ran foul of the French *Vengeur*, her three starboard anchors hooking into the latter's port fore-shrouds and fore-channels. Both ships had squared their yards on coming into contact, had considerable way on them and, with their heads to the north, began a furious close engagement. Unable to open eight lower-deck starboard ports, the crew of the *Brunswick* blew them off by firing their guns through the closed port lids. Rowland Bevan, second lieutenant on board the *Brunswick*, records how, for almost three hours, the two lay together, 'sometimes their guns running into our ports, at other times ours into theirs'. William Kemble, third lieutenant, recalled the two ships 'grinding side by side . . . both on fire at the same time, the dead of both ships being thrown between them. The British and the Sans Culottes lay on each other till the ships wind and separate a little, which gave the bodies to the deep, but they were above the guns'.[21]

At 11 a.m., another French ship, the *Achille*, was seen through the smoke to be bearing down on the port quarter of the *Brunswick*. Crews from the *Brunswick*'s after starboard guns manned her after-most port guns and with double-headed shot brought down the *Achille*'s only remaining mast, the foremast, over her starboard side. Already crippled, with main and mizzen masts also lying across her starboard side, the *Achille* ceased returning fire and struck her colours. With *Brunswick* unable to take advantage of her crippled state, however, the *Achille* re-hoisted her flag and set a spritsail in order to make her escape.

Meanwhile the duel of the *Brunswick* and *Vengeur* was maintained as vigorously as before, except that musket fire had virtually annihilated the upper-deck gun crews of the former. Captain Harvey of the *Brunswick* was wounded three times and was eventually carried below. At 12.45 p.m. the two ships swung and tore apart. The *Vengeur* was by now severely damaged and, in parting, fortunate shooting from the *Brunswick* split her rudder, shattered her stern post and left her leaking severely. At this time the British *Ramillies* approached, adding her fire to that of the *Brunswick* until the French vessel was reduced to a sinking state. The *Ramillies* then made sail to overhaul the *Achille* at about 4.15 p.m. and take her captive.

At 1 p.m. the two original combatants ceased all firing. The *Vengeur* even displayed a British 'Union Jack' over her side in token of submission and as a request for assistance. However, the *Brunswick* lost her mizzen mast at 1.30 p.m., while her other

Fig. 4.iv. Nicholas Pocock's 'Sketch No. 4: The end of the battle'.

Artist's notes: 'A. *Bellerophon*. Fore & Main Topmast gone & much shattered; B. *Valiant*—Main Topsail yard gone & much damaged; C. *Royal Sovereign*. No Masts or yards gone in this Action but much shattered; D. *Russell*. Foretopmast and Gib boom gone; E. *Caesar*, not materially damaged to Outward View but Several shot through her sails; F. *Barfleur*. Masts Rigging & Sails Much Cut; G. *Impregnable*. Ditto; H. *Defence*—Totally dismasted; J. *Invincible*, not much damaged in this Action; K. *Orion* Main Topmast & Main Yard Gone; L. *Queen Charlotte* Fore & Main topmasts gone Yards much wounded hanging up and down. Signal to Wear; M. *Thunderer* Sails and rigging Cut but not very Materially; N. *Gibraltar*. Ditto; O. *Alfred*—ditto. P. *Ramillies* ditto; Q. *Glory*—Foretopmast gone. Otherwise not much disabled; R. *Montagu*. Sails & Rigging much damaged; S. *Royal George* Foremast Main topmast gone, Much disabled; T. *Culloden* much disabled in Sails & Rigging; U. *Marlborough*, totally dismasted; V. *Brunswick* Mizen Mast gone & running before the Wind to get Clear of the French Fleet; W. *Queen*—Main Mast Mizen topmast & fore yard gone Firing on Enemy in Passing; X. *Leviathan*, Foremast & Foreyard much wounded Sails & Rigging much damaged; A. *Pegasus* being ordered to take the *Queen* in Tow; B. *Niger*; C. *Aquilon*, taking the *Marlborough* in Tow.'

masts and rigging were severely damaged. She therefore steered north with the intention of making her way to a British port as best she might. Meanwhile the fore and main masts of the *Vengeur* came down, the latter carrying away the head of the mizzen mast. Rolling with her ports under water, she began filling faster. At 6.15 p.m. she was approached by two British 74s and a cutter which took technical possession of her as a prize although she was sinking too fast for the captors to do more than take off survivors. Estimates of their numbers vary between 150 and 400. The worst wounded had to be left, for she heeled over on her beam ends and sank within a few minutes of the last boat leaving her.

The end of the action

By 12.00 a.m., with the exception of the duel between the *Brunswick* and the *Vengeur*, the heat of the action had passed (See Fig. 4.iv). Most of the other combatants had separated. The British were left with eleven and the French with twelve more or less dismasted ships. However, none of these had struck their colours or, if they appeared to have done so, had rehoisted them, and were striving to make sail on the stumps of mast, and continued to fire on opposing ships. At 1.15 p.m. general firing ceased.

Meanwhile both British and French commanders thought to protect themselves against further attack. Villaret signalled for his van to tack so as to join him and for the rest of his fleet to wear in order to form a new line to leeward. This eventually took shape on the starboard tack, but comprised only eleven[22] of his ships in a line two miles in length. Nevertheless some of his most damaged ships were working their way towards their new line, a number in tow to frigates. Seven French ships lay cut off from their commander-in-chief. By their inability to escape and despite some attempts to resist boarding, six of the French ships were seized by the British: the *Sans-Pareil, Juste, America, Impétueux, Northumberland* and *Achille*. As we have seen, the seventh, the *Vengeur*, sank before she could be made a prize.

More French ships were not taken partly because, as soon as they had disengaged, British ships had begun making emergency repairs. Also, to the frustration of many officers, specific orders to take possession of French ships were lacking.[23] For, seeing the formation of the new French line, Howe was advised against pursuit. Sir Roger Curtis, Howe's flag captain, thought Villaret might intend to capture some of the most damaged British ships. Howe thus signalled to recall distant or chasing ships and to form a line about the *Queen Charlotte* as most convenient. The effect of this signal was to prevent further captures. Thus, for example, two British ships, *Thunderer* and *Culloden*, about to collect two prizes, were recalled. The French fleet was then about three miles (five kilometres) from the *Culloden* and her captain, Isaac Schomberg, after turning back towards Howe, signalled their failure to secure the two prizes and was, in return, directed to stand by them. Wearing again and returning towards the prizes, Schomberg was dismayed to find the prizes had by then drifted within gunshot of the French line.[24]

Curtis's fears proved illusory. Villaret made no attempt to resume action. Even after this was realized, however, still no attempt was made to seize more French ships. After five days and four nights of combat and manoeuvre, Howe, who appeared mentally and physically exhausted, seemed to have come to the end of his resources.[25] After lying at their stations for five nights, younger men too recalled that their 'fatigue was excessive'.[26] For most ships, it was enough to repair and refit.

Villaret was thus able to recover five of his crippled ships, including three without any masts standing,[27] and stood to the north with his whole fleet. By 6.15 p.m., with the exception of a frigate left reconnoitring, the whole of the surviving French fleet, now nineteen ships of the line, was completely out of sight of the British. The latter were, if anything, more badly damaged than their opponents. For it was not until 5 a.m. on 3 June that Howe was able to make sail, when he steered north-east for home. Nine of his fleet put into Plymouth, while the remainder, with the six prizes, anchored at Spithead at 11 a.m. on 13 June.

In both the French and the British fleets, particular ships were singled out for praise or condemnation. On the French side, there was every reason for satisfaction at the conduct of their officers, for many had been recruited into the navy since the revolution. Only twelve had risen in the navy to be lieutenants or sub-lieutenants; nine had been masters of merchant ships, one had been an ordinary seaman, another a boatswain. The courage of most was evident to the British: William Parker watched one captain 'resolutely' putting to the sword seamen who hid from the *Orion*'s broadside. Neverthless two were found wanting. Captain Bompard of the *Montagnard* was charged with deserting the fleet and Captain Gassin of the *Jacobin* with permitting the line of battle to be broken. The charges evoked counter allegations of political motivation and threatened to open the divisions in the French officer corps. Courts martial acquitted Bompard and found Gassin 'guilty but excusable', yet only a change in the political situation in France prevented them having to go before a political tribunal.[28]

Allegations, privately circulated, were just as damaging in the British fleet. Captain Anthony Molloy of the *Caesar* appealed for a court martial to clear himself from an allegation of cowardice. He was exonerated of cowardice but did not survive the obloquy and was dismissed the service in May 1795.[29] For the others, lack of commendation was regarded almost as condemnation. Twenty-five of the admirals and captains who took part received honours or medals. George III further marked the victory by visiting Portsmouth where he presented Howe with a diamond-hilted sword on the deck of the *Queen Charlotte*. Inevitably, those who received less than what they regarded as their due felt slighted. Cuthbert Collingwood of the *Barfleur* was one. Omitted from those who received a gold commemorative medal, he still felt slighted in 1797 when, until honour had been satisfied, he refused receipt of a medal for his part in the battle of Cape St Vincent. Thereupon, he was awarded two! But eight others, including Molloy, received no award at all.[30]

This does suggest that a significant proportion of the British officer corps had performed less well than their admiral demanded. Edward Codrington, serving on board the *Queen Charlotte* in 1794, with the benefit of hindsight, thought Howe 'too forbearing' of the conduct of his captains, observing that St Vincent would never have tolerated what Howe accepted, especially in the actions of 28 and 29 May.[31] Standards of commitment to combat appear to have risen during the French Revolutionary war. Nelson, for example, spoke slightingly of a 'Lord Howe's victory'.[32]

Yet, though contemporaries naturally made comparisons, it is perhaps too facile to compare the performance of officers during the Glorious First of June and later battles. In the confusion of combat, with all its unforeseen accidents, those whose conduct went unremarked were perhaps more unfortunate than undeserving. For much went unnoticed. Much too was taken for granted, especially the professional discipline of the crews of British ships. This emerges strongly from the accounts written by contemporaries that follow. Captain Berkeley, in the *Marlborough*, emphasizes the importance of crew discipline to the quality of British gunnery and defence against boarding; William Parker, midshipman in the *Orion*, reveals the personal relationships between officer and seamen which underlay that discipline; while Rowland Bevan, lieutenant in the *Brunswick*, bears witness to the courage and spirit which infused that discipline. As their words testify, no judgement of performance can be valid which does not incorporate the fighting qualities of the seamen as well as their officers. The achievements of the British navy at the Glorious First of June were a product of the social cohesion that developed on board ships, partly emanating from paternalistic attitudes of the time, but principally from that eternal necessity for seamen to unite in the face of adversity, of which there was no greater experience than the turmoil of battle at sea.

Notes

1. For a survey of recent work on the relationship between navies and political events on shore, see W.S. Cormack, *Revolution and Political Conflict in the French Navy 1789–1794* (Cambridge, 1995), pp. 7–9. Cormack, pp. 275–290, reviews the impact of contemporary French political views on the presentation of events between in May and June 1794.
2. *Sir William Dillon's Narrative of Professional Adventure, 1790–1839*, ed. M. Lewis (2 vols, Navy Records Society, 1953, 1956), vol. I, pp. 128–39; Bouchier, Lady, *Memoir of the Life of Sir Edward Codrington* (2 vols, London, 1873), vol. I, pp. 16–34.
3. Was Pocock the counterpart of James Gillray who had gone to Flanders with official sanction to make sketches prepatory to a major painting by de Loutherbourg on the capture of Valenciennes?

4. See D. Cordingly, *Nicholas Pocock 1740–1821* (London, 1986), pp. 66–76.

5. There were three men named Jonathan Wilkinson mustered on board the *Queen* in 1794. One was from Newcastle, another from Cork and a third from 'Clusley'. The latter place does not exist, but Pleasley is pronounced by locals in a similar way (Plesley) and exists a few miles north-west of Kirkby Woodhouse, near Kirkby-in-Ashfield, Nottingham. This Jonathan Wilkinson was recorded on the books of the *Queen* from 17 January 1793, but had appeared only on 27 January. He was enlisted as an able seaman, and had thus perhaps served on another ship before entering the *Queen*. However, this may not have been the case. He may have been recruited in Nottinghamshire from where he would have taken ten days to reach Portsmouth where the *Queen* was fitting for sea. In this case his rating as 'able', as opposed to 'ordinary' or landsman, may have reflected his physical condition and potential as well as the higher rate of pay attached to that rate that had to be offered to recruit him. PRO, ADM. 36/11365.

6. W.G. Perrin (ed.) *The Naval Miscellany* (Navy Records Society, 1928), vol. III, pp. 157–169.

7. Extracts from this account attributed to Bevan appeared in a memoir of Captain John Harvey in the third volume of the *Naval Chronicle* published in 1800.

8. *The Naval Miscellany*, vol. III, p. 163.

9. With others, the Berkeley-Monckton account has been used and quoted before in O. Warner, *The Glorious First of June* (London, 1961), p. 110.

10. The main source for the manoeuvres between 28 May and 1 June outlined here is W. James, *The Naval History of Great Britain from the declaration of war by France in 1793 to the accession of George IV* (6 vols, 1886 edition). It is noticeable that Pocock often gives slightly different times for signals to James.

11. For Howe's view of these proceedings and his comments on the degree of engagement of individual ships, see Bourchier, *Memoir of . . . Codrington*, vol. I, pp. 22–3.

12. Mr Edward Baker, also in the *Orion* observed that the French 'pointed their guns very high which did a good deal of execution about the rigging, but we fired chiefly at their hulls, as though it best'; quoted in Warner, *The Glorious First of June, p. 128*.

13. Cormack, p. 278.

14. James, vol. I, p. 160. Both Pocock and Parker attribute to Howe a desire for the fleet to have sufficient daylight to complete an

engagement. However, Howe had an additional reason for wanting it: as he told Edward Codrington, then serving on board *Queen Charlotte*, 'he required daylight to see how his captains conducted themselves'. Bourchier, *Memoir of . . . Codrington*, vol. I, p. 30.

15. B. Tunstall, *Naval Warfare in the Age of Sail. The Evolution of Fighting Tactics, 1650–1815* (ed. N. Tracy, London, 1990), p. 209.

16. Thus Berkeley in the *Marlborough* records, for example, changing places with the *Royal Sovereign*.

17. This order differs in some minor respects from that printed in W. James and is taken from Cormack, p. 283. Warner, appendix II, provides a list entitled 'order of sailing' which should be used with caution. It includes, for example, the *Audacious* damaged on 28 May, which had returned to Plymouth before the main action.

18. See Cormack, p. 279, fn. 158.

19. The list of the French ships present here draws upon Cormack who used D. Steel, *Steel's Naval Chronologist of the War* (London, 1802; facsmile reprint London, 1969). But the order that follows differs from Cormack who deduced an order 'partly on the likely position of individual ships given their opponents in the ensuing mêlée'. His deduced order is contradicted by, for example, the court-martial evidence of Captain Molloy of the *Caesar* who maintained the lead ship of the French van was the *Trajan*—see James, vol. I, p. 170. It is also contradicted by the account of Captain Berkeley of the *Marlborough*, who explicitly describes his position in the British line and his opposite number in the French line. The order given here thus adheres to that accepted by James, vol. I, p. 163, and Warner, appendix III, p. 175.

20. Tunstall, p. 209.

21. *The Naval Miscellany*, vol. III, pp. 167–68.

22. Numbers of ships initially forming the French line vary; Pocock says ten; Tunstall eleven.

23. For this frustration, especially on the *Defence*, see the reminiscences of Sir William Dillon in his *Narrative*, vol. I, p. 136.

24. T. Sturges Jackson (ed.) *Logs of the Great Sea Fights, 1794–1805*, (Navy Recording Society, 1899), vol. I, p. 147.

25. Tunstall, p. 210; for the observations of Edward Codrington, who was on board *Queen Charlotte* with Howe, see Bourchier, *Memoir of . . . Codrington*, vol. I, p. 127.

26. Letter of J. Thompson, midshipman, *Barfleur*, to Isaac Thompson, Custom House, Belfast, Ireland, 2 June 1794, printed as a note by Captain Hugh Owen, RN, in *The Mariner's Mirror* 80 (1994), pp. 334–38.

27. These three were *Scipion, Mucius* and *Jemappes.* He also regained *Terrible* and *Républicain* which had lost their main and mizen masts.
28. Cormack, pp. 286–89.
29. For extracts from the court martial see Warner, p. 111. The minutes of the court martial were published in 1796; see James, vol. I, p. 170.
30. For the distribution of honours and medals, see Warner, appendix II; for Collingwood's chagrin, see Warner, pp. 91–101.
31. Bourchier, *Memoir of . . . Codrington,* vol. I, pp. 30, 32.
32. *Logs of the Great Sea Fights,* vol. I, p. 6.

DOCUMENT 4.*i*

NICHOLAS POCOCK'S NOTEBOOK

(Source: National Maritime Museum JOD/12)

Note: Pocock's marginal comments have been added in square brackets []. For clarity, certain abbreviations have been spelt out in full—so that 'TK' has been expanded to 'tack', 'sig.' to 'signal', 'pr' to 'prepare', 'LH' and 'Ld H' to 'Lord Howe' and directions, e.g. 'S by W' to 'south by west'. All other text and brackets are a direct transcription from Pocock's notebook.

Notes taken on board His Majestys Ship Pegasus from May 28 to June 1st 1794

May 28th Wind at South by West a Fresh Breeze & hazy Weather. The British Fleet in the Established order of Sailing in two Columns, on the Larboard Tack Lord Howe leading the Weather Column. On the Weather beam of the fleet Four ships being stationed as 3 miles distant under the Command of Rear Admiral Pasley. Viz. Bellerophon Russell, Thunderer & Marlborough. At 8 AM our advanced Frigates made Signal for a Strange Fleet to Windward. Lord Howe order R A Pasley & Squadron pr Signal to reconnoitre—The Strange Fleet bore down upon us & were soon discovered to be the Enemy consisting of 30 Sail in all. When they reached within about 7 miles of us they began to Haul into a Line on the Larboard Tack. Lord Howe accordingly at 10 Tacked the British Fleet to keep under their lee. At 11 the enemy began Tacking in succession from their Van & from the length of time it took to perform this, Joined to their loss of Ground in backing and filling, being in very bad order of Battle, our Chasing Squadron Gained much on their Rear.

Lord Howe seeing they did (not) mean to come down made the Signal for a General Chase, to Attack or Harrass the Enemys Rear. Soon after to attack as arriving up Lord Howe then tacked in Chase, as did the fleet, to keep under the Lee of the Enemy. The ships of our Chasing Squadron (having passed so near as to fire on the Enemys rear in passing) stood on & tacked, nearly in the Enemys wake, & pushed up towards their Rear. [4 PM] At 5 PM some of their rear ships dropping astern Obliged their Van to shorten Sail, as did the Whole Fleet soon after. At 6 PM the Bellerophon having fetched within of a mile of the

Sternmost ships Lee Quarter began firing upon her & soon made signal for having a mast Wounded which obliged her to keep a little further distant. The Thunderer, Marlborough & Russell came up & fired successively on the Sternmost ship & then dropped into the rear of each other[1] The Leviathan now coming up with a crowd of sail passed the three ships above mentioned, & going between the Bellerophon, & sternmost Ship of the Enemy engaged her closely Lord Howe made Signal for Russell & Marlborough to assist Ships going into Action, Audacious & Gibraltar were now also coming up with a Press of Sail Leviathan seemed closely engaged & the rest of the Advanced ships Attacking successively as before. At 8 [PM] Lord Howe made the General Signal to recall & form a line ahead & astern of him as most convenient. The evening being hazy 'tis possible this signal was not seen by all the Ships, as some of them still remained by the enemy & as long as we could discern the Audacious, she carried a crowd of Sail.[2] Standing up in the Enemys Wake.

The British Fleet got formed tolerably regular in the beginning of the night & carried a smart sail to fore reach & get abreast of the Enemy & the last time we could see them, our Van had extended to Almost the 8th or 9th ship from their Rear.

May 29th Wind still South by West a stiff Breeze & Cloudy Weather the Two Fleets still on starboard tack, and distant about 4 miles   Our Van was abreast the headmost part of the Enemys Centre—As soon as the Admiral could see the position of each Fleet & that the Audacious[3] only had parted Company during the Night He made Signal to Tack in Succession & soon after Signal (34) Viz that he means to pass through the Enemys line & gain the Wind. Our leading Ships when Tacked lay up a little to windward of the rear of the Enemy. The Enemy fearing that some of their Rear might be Cut began to wear, in succession from the van, Run down along their line to the sternmost ship & then hauled to the wind on the Larboard Tack in a line Parallel to ours. Our headmost ships passed so near as to fire on their Rear in passing. the Enemys Van then edged down on our van & seemed inclined to begin a General Action taking their own distance which in general is not very favourable to a British Fleet.[4] This Lord Howe perceiving made signal to Tack in succession at ½ past Eleven which he again annulled, supposing that it might not be completely seen in the Van through the Smoke as Six or Seven were now firing. at ½ past 12 Lord Howe again made Signal to Tack but some unlucky Accident Obliged our Leading Ship to make the Signal of Inability & she soon after Clewed up her Main Topsail.[5] However at 20 minutes past One She again wore, & those astern of her tacked or wore as most convenient. Lord Howe now having repeated the Signal that he meant to pass through the Enemys line and seeing that the Headmost Ships did not Clearly understand his intentions & being impatient to Close with the Enemy, Tacked himself before it came to his turn which Occasioned an Irregularity in our line & left the <u>Queen Charlotte to lead</u> through the Enemys line followed by the Bellerophon & I suppose some others, at ¼ past 2 <u>He</u> was passing between the 5 & 6 Ships from the Enemys rear—<u>When</u> all the rest of our fleet had passed the Rear & to Leeward of the Enemy, Lord Howe made the Signal to Tack & for a General Chase—The Queen, Russell & Invincible made Signal for wanting to lay by, they being much damaged as were several Others of the <u>Fleet</u>. the rear ship of the enemy being totally disabled, lay astern of them in the Midst of Our ships, several of which fired at her in all directions. The French Admiral seeing this ship must be taken if he stood on <u>Wore</u> his fleet in Succession from the Van and rallied in a very Gallant Manner & in Good Order towards Our Fleet, Lord Howe made Signal to wear also Intending I suppose to oppose the Enemys van & cut off the disabled ship & to this purpose bore down himself, but seeing that there were but 2 or 3 ships Near him, and many unable to join him, he made Signal to Form the Line, as most Convenient [29 May 1794] on Starboard Tack & then kept his Wind, While the French Fleet pushed up & carried off their disabled Ship in tow. then Wore in Succession & edged away On Larboard Tack.

Lord Howe remained on the Starboard Tack until the Queen & other disabled Ships were able to Join him & at 20 minutes past 5 He Wore & Edged down after the Enemy. Which had now got to the distance of about 6 miles & there appeared to have hauled their wind. Lord Howe edged down towards them till 7 PM When he hauled to the Wind & then our van was abreast the Rear of the Enemy distant about 6 miles

[31 May 1794] From the 29th at Night, 'till this day at noon a fog Prevented anything of consequence occurring and at intervals <u>only</u>, when the fog cleared. We could see the Enemy. Lord Howe seems determined not to push at them under these <u>Circumstances</u>, for fear that we should not be able to do the business Completely, even if they did allow us to Close, in Consequence of the Obscurity of the Weather,[6] at Noon today what He looked for seemed to approach. the fog cleared away at ½ past one & the Enemy appeared in a line to Leeward 7 miles distant Lord Howe formed the Established Line of Battle hereunto annexed & edged down on a prescribed Course, but the

Enemy keeping from the Wind, prevented our closing near enough At ½ past 6 the Admiral seeing nothing decisive could be done that night made the Signal to haul the Wind on Larboard Tack. The Enemy soon after did the same & then our van was abreast of their Centre. the Frigates from each fleet were placed in the Middle to observe the Motions of their respective Enemies & the two fleets remained nearly in this situation during the night The British however carrying more sail in order to be right abreast of the Enemy by daylight.

June 1st

Wind remains about South by West. Moderate Breeze & Cloudy a Heavy Swell from the westward, at 4 AM saw the Enemy's fleet right abreast of us & distant about 7 miles right to Leeward & all still on Larboard Tack with all Damages from the 29th apparently repaired on both sides, at 5 Lord Howe made signal to bear down, Altering the Course All together at 7 being within 3 miles of the Enemy, the British Fleet hauled their wind together & lay abreast the French which was then waiting to give them Battle. During this interval Lord Howe made the signal (34) that He meant to pass through the Enemys Line & Engage to Leeward N.B. the Captains not being able to effect the specified purpose, are at liberty to act as circumstances require. He then made Signal 36, viz that each ship was to steer for & engage Independently of each other the ship Opposed in the Enemys line, after sufficient time had elapsed for the Several Captains to Consider the present situation of each Fleet And determine what plan was best to pursue in present Serious Situation, Lord Howe bore away & steered for the Montagne, a three decker in the Centre of their Line, the ships of the British fleet each did the same towards his opponent.

At 9 [AM] the enemy began firing on the Headmost part of our Centre, & a Cannonade throughout the centre & van immediately took place & shortly after in most parts of our Rear, the Queen Charlotte for some time desisted firing, She not being able to reach the Montagne, the latter endeavouring to Draw ahead, but the Gallant Charlotte at this Period though fired at by several of the Enemy at the time Set her Top Gallant sails & pushed through the line, with the Signal flying for Closer Action Soon after she had got Close to the Montagnes Quarter Firing into her and was endeavouring to come up alongside, but in coming to the wind after passing her Antagonists Stern, we saw Her Foretopmast Go. which enabled the Montagne of course to shoot ahead & get clear of her. At ½ past 10 we saw the Marlborough Closely Engaged & a French Ship shot up under [her lee quarter (deleted)] & got foul Of Her lee Quarter & having fresh way shoved the

Marlborough round head to wind, when all her sails took aback & she fell on board the Frenchman to Windward. While they were foul of each other another Frenchman got foul of the ship already On board the Marlborough & they all three remained So for some time The Middle Ships Bowsprit at last gave way & the Marlborough got clear & left the two Frenchmen foul of each other We once or twice also had a good opportunity of seeing the Royal Sovereign sticking Close to a Three decker in the van & at last obliging him to bear up & she then chased him to Leeward. The Queen I also had an opportunity sometimes of observing & though it may be improper to particularise where Clouds of smoke kept the chief part of the Fleet totally covered yet there appeared something so superior in her fire to that of the Enemy that I cannot desist mentioning <u>Her</u>. The action continued very violent till Near one o'clock & the ships dismasted seemed to emerge from the Smoke in such a manner that we could not see even who they had engaged last.[7] At about One the French who had it in their power disengaged themselves from the British Fleet 10 Sail appeared to Leeward of ours & Endeavouring to form a line Three sail of the Line had tacked from the Van & were working to Windward & Clear of all our ships About ½ past one Lord Howe seeing that the Enemy had formed the line to Leeward & were standing up towards their disabled ships 8, 9, 10 & 11 (in Sketch 4 [see Fig. 4. iv]) He made signal to Wear together & form a line ahead and astern of him as most convenient The Ships being so disabled 'twas a long time before this was Effected, so that the four disabled ships going before the Wind all the while had got so far to leeward before our ships could prevent them that they joined the above mentioned ten sail.[8] Lord Howe now made signal to secure the disabled ships and Seven were taken possession of

June 1st Continued
The firing having Ceased about 1 PM the following Sketch [see Fig. 4. iv] represents the situation 1.2.3.4.5.6.7. etc. the French ships the 7 first of which being totally dismasted we took possession of, the ship 4 is the Vengeur which sunk the same evening. The ten sail [12.13.14.15.16.17.18.19.20.21] mentioned to have run to Leeward, and are forming a line on the starboard Tack Most of which are in Tolerable Good Order [22.23.24] These are three ships which with the America Tacked from the Enemys van & hauled their wind and got clear, except the latter which was dismasted by the   in the attempt [8.9.11] Two of which are ships of 74 Guns & one a Three Decker totally dismasted & driving before the Wind under their Spritsails &

afterwards Joined their Own Fleet & were carried off. [10.] A Three decker with her Foremast only Standing and running to Leeward Escaped—9

Notes

1. The defensive formation taken by *Thunderer, Marlborough* and *Russell* may be accounted for by reference to the preceding observation that the *Bellerophon*, Rear Admiral Pasley's flagship, had received mast damage; and to the following one relating to Lord Howe's signal for *Russell* and *Marlborough* to assist ships going into action. The journal of Captain Hope, Pasley's flag captain, records this signal as particularly to assist the damaged *Bellerophon*, an interpretation adopted by Captain Berkeley in the *Marlborough* as indicated in his account of the battle that here follows. The *Russell*'s Master also refers to Howe's signal to support 'one another'. For Hope's journal, see *Logs of the Great Sea Fights*, vol. 1, pp. 72, 123.

2. The difficulty of controlling a squadron distant from the fleet in hazy conditions as night fell is here obvious and explains Howe's decision to avoid action late on 31 May so as to have a full daylight on 1 June in order to be able to control his fleet.

3. The *Audacious* had been sufficiently badly damaged in the action to become 'ungovernable'. Her foretopmast and bowsprit were both severely damaged; after refitting all night, she found her foremast was 'both wounded and sprung'. On 29 May she was chased by a French frigate and two corvettes which she drove off. She made Plymouth at 3 p.m. on 4 June. *Logs of the Great Sea Fights*, vol. 1, pp. 99–100.

4. This is presumably a reference to the French preference for firing at masts and rigging in order to disable an enemy, for which they needed to stand off from an opponent. The British on the other hand fired into the hulls, by which they achieved greatest damage by firing at point blank range.

5. Captain Molloy recorded that the *Caesar*'s fore-yard was nearly shot through and her mainstay, fore tack and wather bumpkin block were all shot away. *Logs of the Great Sea Fights*, pp. 78–83.

6. There was evidently general understanding thoughout the British fleet of the necessity for clear visibility and a full day ahead before Howe would commit himself to battle. The thirteen-year-old William Parker comments to the same effect.

7. These references to the smoke that impaired visibility complement

Pocock's realistic pictures of the battle. This degree of obscurity is often not now realized.

8. Had Howe not recalled his ships into a defensive formation, and had the *Vengeur* not sunk, the number of French vessels taken by the British fleet may have been as many as eleven. This figure perhaps better represents the scale of the British victory than the actual number of prizes.

9. Nicholas Pocock went on to depict scenes from the battles of Cape St Vincent, Nile, Copenhagen and Trafalgar and many other noteworthy episodes during the Revolutionary and Napoleonic wars. He exhibited at the Royal Academy until 1815 and, though not so well known in his lifetime, became perhaps the best known marine artist of the war period. He died in 1821.

DOCUMENT 4.*ii*

LETTER FROM JONATHAN WILKINSON TO JOHN CLARK, KIRKBY WOODHOUSE, NOTTS., 2 JULY 1794

(Reproduced from *The Mariner's Mirror* vol. 43 (1957), p. 324, by permission of the Editor)

Spithead 2 July 1794

Honourable Sir,

I make bold to write thieas few lins to You hopeing they will Fiend you and your farther, Brothers and Sisters as well as that leave me Rather Better thanks be to god for it—now Sir to leet you know that I belong to H.M. Ship the Queen of 98 guns[1] as Steward to the Whard Roome and to leet you know Sir that I have bene to the west indies in this ship and to leet you know that I was in the action of the 29 and the first of June against the French fleet Consisting of 29 sail of the line and wead but 26 sail of the line and on the 29 in the morning a bought eight o clock we came to action and we ingaged for Five howers successfull as hard as we Cold fire till at last the french Run from us then we turned two and prapard hower Riging and masts then on the First of June we Came to action a gaine a bought eight o clock in the morning and it lasted till two the same day and to leet you know that hower ship ad to run the gantlet twice throw the french lins and we ad no les than three ships uppon us at one time but by the help of God we made thiem strike to us and in the time of action we sunk two[2] of the French Ships one of 80 guns one of 74 guns and a bought one thousand men sunk with the Ships and in one Ship that we tooke we Cild Right houte five hundred men ded and in hower Ship we ad one hundred and thirty eight Cild and wounded[3] and to leet you know that at the gun that I was Quartred at wead 4 Shot Come in and Cild two men and wounded five do. witch I was wounded in my left harm and in my breast but thanks be to god im a grate deal better and to let you know that hower Captn lost is leg and since dead[4] and the marster of the ship he was Cild Right hout in the time of action and to leet you know that on the 29 of June sume of hower Ships in gaged a bought eight oclock at night but the Rest of hower fleet cud not come to action as the french fleet was to windward of us but we lay uppon the Decks at hower guns all night for two nights and three days as the french fleet Still Ceept in sight and to leet you know that before the action we took 18 ships that

the french ad taken from us and we sunk thieam all and one french brig
of 14 guns we Captred and a Ship of 22 guns and a Cutter of 14 guns[5]
and we took all the french priseners houte and then sunk thieam all but
to leet you know that we have brought 6 Sail of the french line of Battle
Ships into portsmouth harbour whear the kind and Queen as bine to see
thieam and lyke wise to see hower Shatterd Ships. Sir in the time of the
action you would of thort the Ellement ad bene all on fire and the Shot
flying a bought hower Eds 42 pr. And Case Shot and dubbel eded Shot
it was all the same as a hale Storme a bought the Ship but to leet you
know that we are all ready for seea a gaine and I beleve that we shall go
in 6 or Eight days time from heare and to leet you know that admoral
Cardner is hower Commander and I have bene this three years at seea
and as but ad my foot on shore 5 times pleas to be so good as to give
my best respects to Salley Barrows and to Mr. Mills if a live as he is
Sume Releation of mine I ad liked to of forgot im but I hope you will
not forget to spake of me and to leet thieam know whear I am but I
hope this whar will not be long and then I meane to Cum down to See
you plas God to Settel at home witch I make no doupt but what you
wood be glad to see your old Servant once more all tho it is so long
Since I lived with you as a boy you may of forgoot me but I lived with
you when Mearey Meas Seamen was your hous Ceeper.

So I am your Most obt. And Homble sert.

Jno Wilkinson[6]

P.S.
Jno. Wilkinson on board
H.M.ship the Queen of 98 guns
SpitHead portsmouth.

Notes

1. Differences in the level of morale between the crews of ships in
   the British fleet may be distinguishable here. The pride with
   which Wilkinson refers to his ship, the *Queen*, 98, flagship of
   Rear Admiral Gardner, was echoed in references by Pocock and
   Parker. Of the *Queen*, the former observed 'something so superior
   in her fire to that of the enemy' that he could not refrain from
   mentioning her. The latter referred to the cheers prompted on
   board the *Orion* at 'the bold & brave Admiral Gardner' breaking
   the French line on 29 May; he also mentions that the *Queen* was
   cheered on 30 May for her 'gallant behavior' the day before.

2. Wilkinson was here mistaken. Only one French ship sank in consequence of the battle, the 74-gun *Vengeur*.
3. Thirty-six killed and sixty-seven wounded are recorded for the *Queen* in W. Laird Clowes, *The Royal Navy*, vol. IV, p. 226.
4. Captain John Hutt of the *Queen* was made post on 15 January 1783 and died on 30 June 1794.
5. Accounts of the number and nature of the French ships taken or British ships recaptured before the battle are not consistent. Rowland Bevan records three sloops of war being captured and burned. See also W. Laird Clowes, p. 553.
6. Jonathan Wilkinson deserted from the *Queen* on 19 January 1795. PRO, ADM. 36/11363. His desertion may have been linked to a response to this letter. Wilkinson does, after all, hope the war would not last long, express his intention of settling at home, and presumes that his former employer would be glad to see his old servant once more.

DOCUMENT 4.*iii*

LETTER FROM WILLIAM PARKER TO HIS FATHER, 17 JUNE 1794

(Source: National Maritime Museum, PAR/193)

3 O clock—Evening
"Orion" Plymouth Harbour
Tuesday June 17—1794

My dearest Father

No doubt but you are all very much surprised at not having received a long letter from me for 2 or 3 months, and I truly am ashamed of it myself, but I will now give you, as well as I can remember, an account of most particular things that have happened since I last wrote. In the first place, you must know that we paid the ship's company half a years wages on the 18th of April, when I looked in the books & found that I was entered midshipman on the 17 of April, but pray do not mention it to Captain Duckworth. On the 26th April we anchored with the grand fleet & convoy of Indiamen at St Helens; from the 26th April to the 2nd of May it was such calm weather that the fleet was not able to get clear of the land as they got under way, & were obliged to let go their anchors again very often. On the 4th May the convoy parted company & Lord Howe sent Adml Smart [sic[1]] of the Hector & 5 other sail of the line to see them 2 or 3 hundred leagues clear of the land, as the Suffolk 74 & Swift 10 guns were to convoy them to the East Indies. On the 5th May we made the land & our ship & the Latona & Phaeton frigates parted company from the fleet to look into Brest. We did not go clear in ourselves but sent the frigates to look in, as our ship was too large & we did not know the navigation so well, as they had Pilots on board of them. We spoke the Phaeton who told us they counted 19 sail in Brest. On the 18th May we saw 8 strange sail ahead & all the fleet made all the sail they could after them. We supposed them to be the French Cong M Squadron [sic[2]]. At ½ past 10 in the morning, we cleared the ship for action & I assure you we was in a very great bustle & hoisted our colours as did the fleet. At 11 we came up with the chase; it proved to be Admiral McBride's squadron for which reason we shortened sail. On the 19th May we got soundings in 74 fathoms & at 26 minutes past 9 saw Ushant. On the 20th Adml McBride made the signal for Caesar 84, Leviathan 74, Phaeton & Latona, 36 gun frigates, to look into Brest to see if the French fleet were out or not. At half past 3 they joined the fleet again & the Caesar made the signal they were out. We perceived the Latona had a brig in tow which we supposed to be a retaken vessel.

On the 21st of May at 2 in the morning, as it was quite dark we saw several strange lights ahead (as it was our look out ahead) & made the signal to the Admiral; half past 2 cleared ship for action & beat to quarters supposing we were in the midst of the French fleet. At 3 spoke two of them; they proved to be two English vessels captured by the French fleet a few days ago with convoy. The first vessel we spoke still kept on her course, but our marines who were at small arms on the poop soon compelled them to heave to by firing several musket balls at them. They then hove to & we made sail to speak to the Admiral to know what we should do with the ships we had detained. Sir Roger Curtis (Ld Howe's chief captain[3]) desired us to take the prisoners out of them & burn & destroy the vessels. At seven we sent a couple of boats with a Lieutenant in each to burn & destroy them. The brig proved to be the Neptune of Jersey; we found 7 Frenchmen & 2 Englishmen on board her. One of the Englishmen was [the] former mate & was sent into her to convince the French rascals she was a lawful prize; but he was more like a captain than a prisoner on board of her owing to the Frenchmen not knowing how to steer or keep a ships reckoning or anything of seamanship. At a quarter past 7 we set the Neptune on fire & the boats returned with the prisoners. Directly they came on board they were ordered on the quarter deck to be examined by the Captain. They gave us intelligence that the French fleet consisted of 3 first rates, 20 two deckers, most of them 80 guns, and several frigates who left Brest on the 14th supposing that we were looking out for the American convoy. They said they supposed they were about 20 leagues to the windward of us. They gave us intelligence that the Castor & her convoy were captured first by 6 sail of French line of battle ships on the 11th & that they kept the Castor with them & sent a 28 gun ship to convoy the prizes into port. That squadron [i.e. Montagu's], consisting of 6 sail of the line & one frigate, [who] on the 14th parted company from the grand convoy of East Indiamen who retook them again & the 28 gun ship. Admiral Montague then proceeded to the westward after the French squadron & sent the retaken vessels to England. On the 20th they unfortunately fell in with the grand fleet & were captured by them, who sent a frigate & 2 sloops of war to convoy them into one of their ports, when on the 21st we fell in with them as I have mentioned before, but the French frigate & 2 sloops of war got clear of us it being so very dark. Lord Howe considered & thought it the most prudent step he could take to take the prisoners out of them all & burn & destroy the vessels, as it would weaken the fleet by sending men on board of them as we expected to encounter hourly.

We then made sail & left the other 9 re-taken ships in flames & were in great hopes of bringing the French fleet to action very soon & had a favourable wind from the 21st May till the 28th. We took a number of other vessels which were destroyed in the same manner when on the 28th about 8 o clock in the morning we saw a large strange fleet to windward. At 10 the Bellerophon 74 commanded by the bold Adml Paisley went per signal to reconnoitre the strange fleet. At 20 minutes past ten he made the signal that it was an enemy. They were keeping close up to the wind to prevent us getting the weather gage of them as the weather gage is always of advantage. Lord Howe then made the signal to prepare for battle. At half past 11 we could perceive them pretty distinctly formed in one line consisting of 30 sail, 26 of which were of the line of battle & three 3 deckers. We carried a great press of canvas notwithstanding it blew very hard to get to windward of them. We kept bearing up for them & at 4 in the evening the signal was made for Adml Paisley & his squadron to attack the enemy's rear. At 8 oC Adml Paisley got within gun shot of the enemy's rear & gave them a very warm & fierce reception which the enemy returned with great vivacity. The whole of our fleet were now carrying all the sail they could to get up with & bring the French fleet to action. At 9 we beat to quarters & were in perfect readiness to pour a broadside in to any of the enemy's ships we could bring our ship to bear on. The night being very dark it afforded a grand and awful sight from the flash of the guns. At half past 9 the firing ceased owing to the wind blowing very hard & a rough sea[4] preventing our ships from getting up with & bringing the enemy to action which much dissatisfied our officers & the ships company.

We continued at our quarters all night & the next morning we perceived the enemy formed in a line & bore up after them. At half past 7 the van of our fleet engaged our enemy but no execution was done being at a great distance. A quarter before ten they began firing at our van, which presently brought on a general engagement, which was kept up by every ship as they came abreast of the enemy. The enemy fired chiefly at our rigging trying to dismast us & we at their hulls, which we thought the best way of weakening them.[5] It was surprising to see with what courage our men behaved. There were even some of them so eager that they jumped up in the rigging to huzza, & Captn Duckworth hauled them down by the legs (I mean the brave fighting cool Duckworth). We had not fired two broadsides before an unlucky shot cut a poor man's head right in two and wounded Jno Fane & four other youngsters like him very slightly. The horrid sight of this poor man I must confess did not help to raise my spirits. At 12 the bold & brave Admiral Gardner according to custom broke their line upon which our ships company gave three hearty cheers at their quarters. We then passed the whole of the French line and were exposed to a very smart & close cannonading from the enemy which we returned with very great warmth. We then lay to to repair our rigging a little when, seeing their sternmost ship of 80 guns a little way ahead, we bore up for her and running close under her weather quarter let fly a broadside into her, which raked her fore & aft, & so effectually that it made the Frenchmen according to custom race from their quarters & huddle together down below & the French Captain was the only person seen upon deck which he walked very resolutely & put every one of his men to sword whom he saw fly.[6] We then came round upon her beam & with our large guns poured another broadside into her with good effect when unluckily some [? shot] coming from her into our lower gun deck killed two men & wounded five others. The Barfleur then came in between us & fired at her for some time notwithstanding which & the fire from several other ships she would not strike, & I believe that she must & did go down; she was so wrecked & disabled that at half past 4 we hauled off to repair our damages.

During the whole action of this day we had only 3 men killed & 20 slightly wounded. During this time some of our ships who had not been in action before that day began a smart action with the enemy which continued till about 9 when they hauled off & we gained the weather gage so that it was now in our power to bring the rascals to battle when we pleased. On the 30th it was such foggy weather that we could see none of the enemy's fleet and very few of our own. At 8 it cleared up a little & at 11 we gave the Queen, Admiral Gardner, 3 cheers for her gallant behaviour on the 29th. On the 31st it was still foggy weather so that we could not see any of the enemy though we supposed they were about 3 leagues to the leeward of us. At 2 it cleared up & became pleasant sunshiny weather and we saw the French about 7 miles to leeward of us, & we bore down upon them & at 6 beat to quarters as we expected to bring them to action every hour.

Lord Howe always likes to begin in the morning & let us have a whole day at it. The next morning early the signal was made to form the line of battle. We beat to quarters & got up sufficiently of powder & shot to engage the enemy; the enemy also formed their line to leeward. Upon our making observations on the enemy's fleet we found that one of their 3 deck ships were missing but counted 28 sail of the line which was two more than they had on the 29th May.[7] We supposed the Bay squadron had joined them & the ship that we had disabled on the 28th had bore up for Brest or sunk & some thought the Audacious must have taken one of them & took her away from the fleet as she was missing the 30th May.[8] But the best joke was that the French Commander-in-Chief had the impudence to say to those ships who joined him that he had thrashed us on the 29th completely & that he only wanted to have another little dust with us before he should carry us all into Brest.[9] Our fleet was formed & we only waited to get near enough to the enemy to begin. At eight the action began & the firing from the enemy was very smart before we could engage the ship that came our turn to engage, as every ship is to have one because our line is formed ahead, & theirs is formed also. Suppose their first or leading ship is a 100 guns, & ours a 74, our ship must engage her.[10] I believe we were the ninth or tenth ship, our lot fell to an 80 gun ship, so we would not waste our powder & shot by firing at other ships, tho' I am sorry to say they fired very smartly at us, and unluckily killed two men before we fired a gun, which so exasperated our men that they kept singing out—"For God's sake Brave Captain let us fire! Consider Sir two poor souls are slaughtered already"—but Captn Duckworth would not let them fire till we came abreast of the ship we were to engage, when Captn Duckworth cried out "Fire my Boys. Fire", upon which our enraged Boys gave them such an extraordinary warm reception that I really believe it struck the rascals with the panic.[11] The French ever since the 29th (because we so much damaged one of their ships) called us the little Devil & the little Black Ribbon as we have a black streak painted on our side.[12] They made the signal for three or four of their ships to come down & sink us, & if we struck to them to give us no quarter. But all this did not in the least dishearten our ships company & we kept up a very smart fire, when some of the enemy's masts & yards went over their side, which we give credit for some of our doing. The smoke was so thick that we could not at all times see the ships engaging ahead & astern.[13] Our main top mast & main yard being carried away by the enemy's shot, the Frenchmen gave 3 cheers, upon which our ships company, to shew they did not mind it, returned them the cheers & after that gave them a furious broadside.[14] About this time a musket ball came & struck Captn Duckworth between the bottom part of his thumb & finger but very slightly so that he only wrapped a handkerchief about it, & it is now almost quite well.

But to proceed with my account, at about ten the Queen broke their line again & we gave 3 cheers at our quarters, & now we engaged whichever ship we could beat. A ship of 80 guns, which we had poured 3 or 4 broadsides into on the 29th May, we saw drawing near on our lee quarter to fire into us, which ship our ships company had a great desire to have made strike to us on the 29th & now quite rejoiced at having an opportunity of engaging her again, gave three cheers at their quarters & began a very smart firing at their former antagonist. Their firing was not very smart, though she continued to send a red hot shot into the Captn's cabin where I am quartered, which kept rolling about & burning every body, when gallant Mears our first Lieutenant took it up in his speaker-trumpet & threw it overboard. At last, being so very close to her, we supposed her men had left their quarters as Frenchmen do not like close quarters. She bore down to leeward of the fleet being very much disabled. The signal was made for Gibraltar & Culloden to cover us from the fire of the enemy as we were very much disabled. Our ships company were employed in cutting away the wreck some of which was on fire, which we soon put out by drawing water with our fire buckets.

The ships that were not disabled still engaged the enemy. At half past one the Brunswick's mizzen and main masts were shot away & she went to leeward of the fleet & we were very much afraid she would have been taken. At last we saw her bear up & set all the sail she could, but there was no possibility of her getting into our line again. At two the firing ceased but we did not know whether the action was over or no. We were employed in getting ready for engaging & were very close to the Admiral & perceived he had lost both his fore & main top masts in the action and two or three of our own ships totally dismasted. There were seven of the Frenchmen also dismasted, but some of them had still their colours flying. We saw one of them hoisting a little small sail & edging down and she would soon have joined her own fleet had not Mr Mears seen it and let fly an 18 pounder right astern of her which made her strike her colours & hoist English & strike her sail also. Captn Duckworth ordered no more guns to be fired at her & then we had it in our power to say that she struck to the "Orion". The French fleet then ran away like cowardly rascals & we made all the sail we could. Lord Howe ordered our ships that were not very much disabled to take the prizes in tow & our own dismasted ships who were erecting jury masts as fast as possible. But I forgot to tell you that the ship which struck to us was so much disabled that she could not live much longer upon the water but gave a dreadful reel & lay down on her broadside.[15] We were afraid to send any boats to help them because they would have sunk her by too many poor souls getting into her at once. You could plainly perceive the poor wretches climbing over to windward & crying most dreadfully. She then righted a little and then her end went down gradually & she sunk. She after that rose again a little, and then sunk so that no more was seen of her. Oh! my dear Father! When you consider of five or six hundred souls destroyed in that shocking manner it will make your very heart relent.[16] Our own men even were a great many of them in tears & groaning. They said, God bless them, Oh that we had come into a thousand engagements sooner than so many poor souls should be at once destroyed in that shocking manner. I really think it would have rent the hardest of hearts.

We then bore away for England & Lord Howe sent a frigate with Sir Roger Curtis with dispatches, by which I sent my ship letter. On the 16th we made the land & parted company from Lord Howe to go under command of Admiral Graves to Plymouth. There were seven other sail of the line who came into Plymouth with us but none of the prizes. We went alongside the hulk directly &, before we could get properly lashed to her, Mr Lane was on board and took me & his son & Franks & Baker to Coffleet. It is really impossible to describe the kind attention of Miss Lane & the family. I met there Mrs Collins, the widow of poor Captn Collins, who was in the navy. She has been married twice & had her daughter by her first husband with her, a very pleasant amiable girl. Captn Duckworth gave orders for us to return on Monday which we did & I have taken the earliest opportunity of writing to you. Mrs Collins was so kind as to ask us to dine with her on Thursday to meet Mrs & Miss Lane & Family & to go to the Long Room at night & return on board the next morning. Pray do you know any Captain Lane of the navy. He says he knows our family. When I was at Coffleet I received news by Mr Lane who rode into Plymouth, which made me so uneasy & almost broke our brave Captain's heart. Most of our brave boys have undone all the good they ever did. Last Friday night they contrived to smuggle a great deal of liquor into the ship &, with the joy of having returned safe into port & of the victory, most of the ships company got so drunk that they mutinied. They said they would have liberty to go ashore. They released the prisoners out of irons. Every officer belonging to the ship was sent for. The Captain almost broke his heart about it.

Seven of the ringleaders were seized by the officers & twenty other men. They were put in irons & the next morning, when they were told of their night's proceedings, they wept like children. The twenty were punished with [blank] lashes each, & the seven were kept in irons & would have been if tried by a court martial, but Captain Duckworth had them before him to-day & said that as he was of a forgiving nature he gave them into the hands of the ships company, that he restores them to them with love for the services they had done him.[17] Pray do not mention any thing about it to Captain Duckworth.

I think it would be very proper for my sisters to make Miss Lane a present. I hope it will not be long before I shall have the pleasure of seeing you. Tell my mother pray that I received her agreeable letter. Give my duty to her & love to my brothers & sisters &, believe me, your dutiful and happy son

William Parker.[18]

My dearest Father, may I request & ask you a favour to get a subscription made for the wife & children of George Graham, a gallant unfortunate seamen who was slaughtered in the engagement on the first of June in a manner too shocking to mention to a tender hearted parent. This poor man, whom I now so much lament, when alive taught me several [lessons] of seamanship, which if I ever forget will be the greatest ingratitude & of course render me unworthy of being called your son.

Notes

1. In fact Admiral Sir George Montagu.
2. Cancale Squadron? Six French ships of the line and two rasées were based at Cancale to support an invasion of the Channel Islands.
3. That is, Captain of the Fleet or flag captain of the *Queen Charlotte*.
4. The wind and sea are not usually referred to as reasons why the fighting came to an end on 28 May.
5. Pocock also refers to the difference between the French and British preferences for inflicting damage on their opponents. After the battle, noting that only four of the British ships as opposed to thirteen of the French were dismasted, Villaret-Joyeuse assumed the British gunners were trained to aim high. The British practice of firing alternately high then low when in close combat is well described by Rowland Bevan in his account of the *Brunswick*'s engagement with the *Vengeur*. *Naval Miscellany*, vol. III, p. 163.

6. The determined fighting quality of some of the French officers and seamen on 1 June was noteworthy. One observer on the *Royal George* noticed one French ship fire into another that had surrendered; see *Logs of the Great Sea Fights*, p. 57. But Villaret-Joyeuse blamed the outcome of the battle on the inexperience or incapacity of his officers. Only twelve of the French captains in the battle of 1 June had risen in their royal navy. See Cormack, p. 285.

7. The badly damaged 110-gun *Révolutionnaire* had escaped after the action of 28 May and the French fleet had been joined on 30 May by three ships of the line under Rear Admiral Nielly.

8. The contemporary difficulty of communicating between and controlling ships during and after battle is here self-evident. The *Audacious* had left the British fleet on 29 May, but she was not missed by observers on the *Orion* until 30 May.

9. The attribution of this 'joke' to Villaret-Joyeuse will probably never be verified. Nevertheless it suggests communication between the fleets, probably by conversation with prisoners after the final battle.

10. In fact Howe allowed some ships to change places in the British line before the action began. Captain Berkeley records that the *Marlborough*, for example, changed places with the *Royal Sovereign* before the battle.

11. The importance of discipline to the firing of guns is here self-evident. The impact of the first broadside on an enemy crew largely unaccustomed to battle must have had an unnerving effect on their fighting capability.

12. The nick-names given to the *Orion* by the French seem again to suggest relatively free communication between the fleets.

13. Like Pocock, Parker here emphasizes the extent and density of the smoke generated by the gunfire.

14. Note the practice within the French as well as the British fleet of giving three cheers. Whether the cheers were led by officers or particular members of the crew is uncertain. In this case, the cheering seems to have been spontaneous.

15. This was the *Vengeur du Peuple*.

16. Estimates of the number lost in the *Vengeur* vary. French estimates, reinforcing the image of heroic sacrifice generated after the battle, correspond with this one of Parker's. However Captain John Harvey of the *Brunswick* reported 250 saved, the *Culloden* saved about 300 and the *Alfred* took on board 213. British estimates of losses thus tend not to exceed 300. O. Warner, *The Glorious First of June*, p. 87; *Logs of the Great Sea Fights*, vol. 1, pp. 105, 148.

17. The impulse to drink, both to celebrate and to relieve the trauma of battle, is understandable. The containment of the subsequent mutiny reflects the ability of Duckworth to manage his crew, a quality rarely so well illustrated as here.

18. William Parker became a lieutenant in September 1799 and a captain in 1801. He was a rear admiral in 1830 and a full admiral in 1851. He died in 1866.

DOCUMENT 4.iv

LETTER FROM ROWLAND BEVAN, 2ND LIEUTENANT OF THE *BRUNSWICK*, TO T. MORGAN ESQ, SWANSEA

(Source: National Maritime Museum JOD/12)

Dear Sir, we sailed from St Helens the 2d May with the East–West India fleets, in company with 33 sail of the line and several frigates. The 4th, 7 sail of the line parted company with us to proceed with the convoys. Lord Howe with 26 sail stood over to the coast of France which we saw the next morning. Sent 3 frigates and a line of battle ship to look into Brest; found the French fleet were there. We then stood to the westward after our convoy. The 19th we made Ushant. The Admiral sent two line of battleships and two frigates to look into Brest; found the French fleet had sailed. Spoke an American ship; the captain informed us that the Fleet had sailed the 9th May and had steered to the westward under press of sail.[1] Lord Howe then made the signal to steer WNW which we did until the 27th. We were then near 200 leagues to the South [of] the Lizard. From the 19 to 27th fell in with several ships that the French fleet had taken, 3 sloops of war, all which were burnt.[2] From the latter we got intelligence that the French fleet was to the westward. The 27th in the evening we tacked and stood to the SE; on the 28th in the morning one of our lookout frigates made the signal for a strange fleet. We then spoke an American who had passed through the fleet. He informed us that the fleet to [windward] of us was the French fleet consisting of 26 sail of the line and several frigates. Lord Howe then made the signal for a general chace and the fleet to prepare for action. About ½ after 7 some of our flying squadron made the signal that they could come up with the chace. The Admiral then made the signal to harrass the enemy's rear. A partial action took place during the first part of the night. At daylight on the 29th we perceived the enemy's fleet in a line to windward. Lord Howe made the signal to form the line on the starboard tack as most convenient, the enemy being on the same tack. At 10 Lord Howe made the signal to tack in succession, at the same time signal for general chace. The van of our fleet fetching very near their rear, the enemy gave them their fire which our ships did not return. About 11 the van of the French fleet wore, immediately afterwards the whole of their fleet did the same and formed the line on the starboard tack, edging down in succession on

93

our fleet. About 12 or after, their van began to engage our van, so on to the centre, but at too great a distance.

½ after one Lord Howe made the signal for our fleet to tack, which they did, led by Captain Molloy in the Caesar, and, supported gallantly by the van & centre, broke the enemy's rear. This brought on a general cannonade from the whole of our fleet on the enemy's rear during which time two of the enemy's ships were dismasted. The manoeuvre gave us the wind of the enemy, they being obliged to bear up to join their disabled ships. This evening it grew hazy & continued until 31st about noon when it cleared away a little. About 4 the fog cleared away and we saw the French fleet about 8 or 9 miles to leeward of us. Lord Howe made the signal to form the line on the larboard tack, which was done. He then made the signal for the van to prepare to engage the van of the enemy. He then made the signal to come to the wind on the larboard tack in a close order of battle in which position we lay all night. The morning of June the first, different manoeuvres till about ½ past nine. Lord Howe made the signal for each ship to engage her opponent and immediately bore down in a most gallant manner. The Brunswick, being the second astern, kept close to him. We were very much cut up going down, as they lay too to receive us. We did not fire a single gun until we were within point blank shot.[3] 10 minutes after ten we lay the Vengeur, an 84,[4] alongside, sometimes their guns running into our ports, at other times ours into theirs.[5] We lay in this situation until one o'clock when she struck to us, our mizen mast being gone, our other masts shot to pieces, not a boat that would swim. In this situation we were left to the mercy of the sea.[6] On examining the ship, we found we had lost 10 of our lower deck ports, 2 guns dismounted, and the ship totally disabled. We had 40 men killed and 113 wounded.[7] Our brave captain lost his right arm. I had the misfortune to be wounded in my left eye, my breast and both legs. The former wounds are much better, but my left leg still remains in a state of uncertainty whether I shall lose it or not.

The French fleet, being disabled, wore and ran to leeward. We disabled could not join our own fleet and was obliged to run before the wind, when we left the fleet.[8]

Notes

1. Reports of when the French fleet actually sailed vary. The French accounts agree it was on 27 Floréal (16 May).

2. The French vessels and captures taken and destroyed prior to the juncture of the fleets are obscure. Laird Clowes, p. 553, records a 10-gun cutter *Courier* taken and scuttled, and the 20-gun *Républicain* taken and burned, each on the 25 May. William Parker's account makes clear that a number of vessels were taken and burned before 28 May.

3. The French practice of shooting at the rigging and British gun discipline are both re-emphasized here.

4. The *Vengeur* was nominally a 74, not an 84 as stated by Bevan.

5. For the manoeuvres that took the *Brunswick* alongside the *Vengeur*, see the account by Bevan and Kemble in *Naval Miscellany* (Navy Records Society, 1927), vol. III, pp. 159–69. Bevan also there records the method of British gunnery at close quarters and its effect, the various forms of langridge—raw ore and sulphur—used by the French, and the accuracy of small arms fire.

6. Bevan's account printed in the *Naval Miscellany*, vol. III, records the help provided to the *Brunswick* by the *Ramillies* at this stage in the battle. The *Ramillies* was captained by Henry Harvey, brother of John Harvey, captain of the *Brunswick*, and the show of fraternal assistance evidently did much for morale in the *Brunswick*.

7. The *Brunswick* had the biggest casualty list in the British fleet; 44 killed and 114 wounded in the three actions, 28 May–1 June 1794. It included Captain John Harvey who died after the battle. Laird Clowes, vol. IV, p. 226.

8. Rowland Bevan was promoted to commander on 6 July 1794 and became a captain in June 1808. He died in 1836.

DOCUMENT 4.v

REPORT OF CAPTAIN GEORGE CRANFIELD BERKELEY AND LIEUTENANT JONATHAN MONKTON TO ADMIRAL EARL HOWE, 6 JUNE 1794

(Source: British Library Add Mss 23,207 ff. 67–70)

Marlborough at Sea, June 6th 1794

My Lord

I shall endeavour to obey your Lordship's Directions in reporting the Proceedings and Observations of His Majesty's ship under my command during the Actions of the 28th, 29th of May and the 1st of this Month.

On the 28th the Signal being made for Admiral Pasley's division to reconnoitre the Enemy, the Marlborough made sail and came up with the Enemy's Rear and when the Signal was made to attack their Rear, opened an occasional Fire upon the Sternmost Ship; But as I imagined it was not your Lordship's Intention to have the Advanced Ships engaged before the Rest of the Fleet were ready to support them, I did not pass my Admiral, a Measure which I found myself justified in, by the subsequent Signal of Recall, and as the Bellerophon had made the Signal of Distress I thought it my Duty to stay by her; The Leviathan and Audacious were at that time closely engaged with the Sternmost Ship and I saw very plainly about half past Eight o'Clock, the Frenchman's Mizen Top on Fire, soon after an Explosion took Place and her Mizen Mast fell; She then paid round off and kept a weak Fire upon the Audacious until she came into the Rear of our Fleet when she struck and was taken Possession of by the Audacious,[1] the Thunderer bore up to give her Assistance and therefore I did not think it necessary to remain but followed the Bellerophon's Light.[2]

At Day Light on the 29th the Signal was made to form as most convenient and I took my Station next to the Bellerophon and Charlotte and in this Situation engaged the Enemy. When we had passed the last Ship who was much disabled I tack'd and stood after the Charlotte, who was the only Ship ahead of us at that time and upon her tacking again and making the Signal for forming as most convenient, I took my Station astern of her. But being hail'd by the Valiant whose signal was made I gave Way to her and stood on to the Queen and Invincible who were both very much crippled and whose Protection I imagined was your Lordship's principal Object.

On the 1st of June at Eight o'Clock I chang'd Places with the *Royal Sovereign*,[3] by which Means I became the Sixth Ship in our line and therefore when the Signal was made to engage each Ship his Opponent and break the Line I bore up and gave strict Charge not to fire a Gun until I ordered, which was most implicitly obeyed.[4] Observing my Opponent which was an Eighty four Gun Ship[5] with two Yellow Streaks[6] and I am since inform'd is the Impetueux had his Main Topsail aback, I trimmed my Sails exactly the same and running under his Stern gave him my Fire and luff'd up close under his Quarter and kept engaging him for about twenty Minutes when from some damage to his Steerage or from some other Cause he paid round off and dropt with his Bowsprit over our Quarter where he lay exposed to a very heavy Raking Fire which we kept up. Every Creature was drove from his Decks and some of my Men boarded him but were call'd back.[7] I had now the Satisfaction to see all his Masts go over the Side and as we had not at this time received much Damage, I was in Hopes to have taken up my Place in the Line again. At this Moment a Seventy-Four who was astern of the Impetueux attempted to weather and rake us; But the Judgement of the Officers who had the Direction of the Guns gave him so severe a Reception that he dropt on board of his Consort's Quarter and then luffing up boarded the Marlborough upon the Bow. The Steadiness of our Troops[8] and the good Use we made of the Guns and Carronades prevented his availing himself of his Situation; Although it was by no Means a favorable one for him, for being Stern on he was rak'd very much by our Guns. In a few Minutes I had the Pleasure of seeing this Ships Masts follow the Example of the other and they both lay without firing a Gun, or without any Colours, which makes me suppose they had struck as not a Soul was upon Deck to answer; and what confirmed me in this Opinion afterwards, when we were dismasted we lay alongside the Impetueux within Half-Pistol Shot without any Attempt being made against us; until our own Fleet came up and took Possession of them.

I now attempted to back off from the two Wrecks and unfortunately accomplish'd it just as the French Admiral came under our Stern, who back'd his Main Topsail and rak'd us, by which he did us considerable Damage and carried away our Three Masts; We however were luckily in such a Situation as to be able to fire upon him, and he past [sic] us. It was from this Ship I received my Wound and therefore the Remainder is the Account of my First Lieutenant

G Berkeley

At the time Captain Berkeley was obliged to quit the Deck, we were still on board, But backing clear of our Opponents; Our Masts being then Shot away by the Three-Decker under our Stern, carried away the Ensign Staff and deprived us of hoisting any Colours for a few Minutes; I ordered the Wreck to be clear'd away from the Colour Chest and spread an Union Jack at the Spritsail Yard and a St George's Ensign on the Stump of the Fore Mast. But perceiving that the latter was mistaken by some of our ships for the Tricoloured Flag, I ordered the Flag to be cut off.[9] At this Time we were laying along side the Impetueux within a Pistol Shot and finding that she did not return a Gun and perceiving she was on Fire, I ordered our Ship to cease firing at her and suffer'd them quietly to extinguish the Flames which I could easily have prevented with our Musquetry. I now ordered the Larboard Yard Arm of the Spritsail to be loosed as the other was shot away, and the Boats Sails to be set in the Boats on the Booms[10] and clear'd away the Wreck in Order to get the Ship under Command, if possible. By this time the Rear of the Enemy's Fleet was coming up and perceiving that they must range close to us,[11] and being determined never to see the British Flag struck, I ordered the Men to lye down at their Quarters to receive their Fire and to return it afterwards if possible; but being dismasted she roll'd so deep that our Lower Deck Ports could not be opened. The Event was as I expected, the Enemy's Rear pass'd us to Leeward very close and we fairly run the Gauntlet of every Ship which could get a Gun to bear; but luckily without giving us any Shot between Wind and Water or killing any Men except two, who imprudently disobey'd their Officers and got up at their Quarters.[12] Two of their Ships who had tack'd now came to Windward of us and gave us their Fire, upon which one of the Hulks hoisted a National Jack but upon our Firing some Guns at her she hauled it down again and a Three Decker having tack'd also, stood towards us with a full Intention, I believe, to sink us if possible,[13] The Royal George however who I suppose had tack'd after her, came up and engaging her very closely, carried away her Main and Mizen Masts and saved the Marlborough from the intended Close Attack of this Ship who immediately bore up for the Body of the French Fleet to Leeward. I then made the Signal for Assistance on a Boat's Mast; but this was almost instantly shot away; At Five the Aquilon took us in Tow and our Fleet standing towards us, we joined them very soon afterwards.

Jn°. Monkton 1st Lieut.

Thus my Lord I have endeavoured to give you a detail'd an Account as the Observations of myself and Officers can furnish and I should feel myself ingrateful to the Officers and Men if I did not recommend them to your Lordship's notice.[14]

The perfect Discipline and well-directed Fire which the Officers kept up at their Quarters; could only be equall'd by the Coolness, Obedience and Bravery of the Men, and the very trying and critical Juncture in which Lieutenant Monkton took the Command of the Ship and kept the British Flag triumphant until the Victory was decided, demands my utmost Praise.

I am
with great Esteem and Regard
Your Lordships
Devoted Humble Servant
G Berkeley[15]

Notes

1. The *Révolutionnaire* was not of course taken by the *Audacious*.
2. This account of the action of 28 May by Berkeley sounds a note of self-justification. Had Berkeley known that the French *Révolutionnaire* was not taken, it probably would have sounded even more defensive. Could the attack of Pasley's squadron have been better managed, either by Howe from a distance or by Pasley from the damaged *Bellerophon?* Any answer to the question must bear in mind the glowering presence of the French fleet and the failing light that left the whole of the British fleet in ignorance of what happened to *Audacious* and *Révolutionnaire*.
3. Howe permitted ships to change places so as to match ships of roughly equal force in the French line. The exchange of the *Marlborough* with the *Royal Sovereign* permitted the latter to engage the 110-gun *Terrible.*
4. Overall control of the guns, as on the *Orion*, was kept by the ship's captain, with whom discipline in firing was clearly a point of pride and part of his management of the crew. Note Berkeley's

concluding commendation of his officers for their 'perfect discipline and well-directed fire . . . at their quarters'.

5. The *Impétueux* was nominally a 74-gun ship, not an 84.

6. Note the identification of the *Impétueux* by the 'two yellow streaks'. The *Orion* was identified by the French by her black streak. There was no uniform warship appearance at this time.

7. In boarding, control over the seamen and marines or soldiers was as important as discipline in cavalry.

8. Howe had a regiment of infantry in the fleet on account of the shortage of marines.

9. The mistake of the St George's ensign for the French republican Tricolour was probably the product of the enveloping smoke. British captains were generally very conscious of the dangers of firing into their own ships. The British ships responsible for this 'friendly fire' were the *Gibraltar* and *Culloden*. See *Logs of the Great Sea Fights*, p. 130.

10. The expedient of setting sails on ship's boats when all three masts were shot away is here adopted as though conventional practice. Monkton had considerable experience, having become a lieutenant in 1777. He became a rear admiral in 1814.

11. An extract from Monkton's personal account of the battle was printed in Laird Clowes, vol. IV, p. 320, fn. 1, and contains some anecdotes of his conduct and of the state of the crew's morale. The Marlborough was in real danger when it lay dismasted as the ships forming the rear of the French fleet approached to fire in turn.

12. The deaths of the two seamen no doubt emphasized to those who survived them the importance of implicit obedience during the battle.

13. When severely disabled, both *Brunswick* and *Marlborough* found themselves engaging more than one opponent simultaneously. In view of the roughly equal number of ships in each fleet at the beginning of the battle, and the greater number of French vessels that were dismasted, some British ships may have neglected to closely engage opponents, allowing them to combine together against single British vessels.

14. The *Marlborough* lost twenty-nine killed and ninety wounded in the three actions. She suffered the second highest number of casualties after *Brunswick*. The *Queen* had more killed—thirty-six.

15. George Berkeley took a full part in the operations of the Channel fleet during the remainder of the Revolutionary War and became a rear admiral in 1799. He rose to the rank of full admiral in 1810 and died in 1818.

5

The Man who Missed the Grain Convoy

Rear Admiral George Montagu and the Arrival of Vanstabel's Convoy from America in 1794

Michael Duffy

And whereas Intelligence has been received that a very large and valuable Fleet of Merchant Ships may be shortly expected from America under convoy of a French Squadron . . . and whereas the attempting to intercept the same is an object of the most urgent importance to the success of the present war, Your Lordship is hereby required and directed to give orders to the Rear Admiral (to be detached to a certain distance with the East India Convoy as aforesaid) after performing that service to cruize, for such time as you may think proper, from Cape Ortegal to the Latitude of Belle Isle, for the sake of intercepting the same accordingly, Or you will make a detachment of any other part of the Fleet under your command for the performance of this service, as to your Lordship may appear most adviseable.[1]

Such were the Admiralty's instructions to Earl Howe as he prepared to take the Channel Fleet to sea in April 1794. Throughout the earlier part of the year the British government had been kept informed by its consular officials on the east coast of the United States of the build-up of French merchant shipping in American ports. From Norfolk, Virginia, Consul Hamilton reported on 6 and 9 January the presence of about thirty large French ships 'richly laden' from St Domingo and another thirty at Baltimore loaded with flour but detained in the river by the ice. Between 19 and 23 February the consuls announced a sudden flurry of French activity with the arrival in the Chesapeake of an 80- and a 74-gun ship of the line, three 40-gun frigates, two corvettes, a brigantine and an armed storeship, which had left France on 25 December. There was also a report of two more 74s going to New York.[2] Consul Bond at Philadelphia, seat of the federal government, added that besides a new envoy to the American Republic, the French squadron had brought with them $1 million[3] of treasure which they deposited in the Bank of the United States to buy flour and other provisions to be loaded on the ships in the Chesapeake and convoyed to France. His initial estimate was that at least three weeks would be needed to procure the necessary supplies.[4] With the French Republic pressed by food shortages it was clearly making a major effort to procure relief from America as well as to rescue the capital and produce tied up in the marooned ships of the West Indian trade.

When these last despatches were received in London on 8 April, the Admiralty added the responsibility for intercepting this convoy to the tasks of the Channel Fleet in its forthcoming cruise. Howe had to provide an escort across the Bay of Biscay for a large convoy for the East Indies and any other trade ready to sail, and he was to cruise off Ushant to protect trade entering or leaving the Channel, to intercept enemy warships, privateers and trade, and to ensure the security of the British Isles against invasion.[5] He accordingly entrusted the task of intercepting the convoy to the commander who would escort the East Indies convoy across the Bay, Rear Admiral George Montagu.

Montagu was the most junior of Howe's flag-officers having only just been promoted to Rear Admiral of the Blue on 12 April. He came from a naval family. His father John Montagu was an admiral and his brother James was shortly to be killed when captain of the 74-gun ship of the line *Montagu* at the battle of the Glorious First of June. Born on 12 December 1750, he was placed in the Royal Naval Academy at Portsmouth at the age of thirteen and in 1766 joined the 50-gun *Preston* under Captain Alan Gardner on the Jamaica station. In 1771 he was promoted lieutenant and thereafter advanced rapidly under the patronage of his father who in 1770 was made a Rear Admiral and in 1771 given command of the North American station whither he took his son George in his flagship. In 1773 his father appointed him commander of the *Kingfisher* sloop and in 1774 post-captain of the 20-gun *Fowey* in which in December 1775 he captured the first American warship taken during the War of Independence, the *Washington* of ten guns and ten swivels. In March 1776 he supervised the embarkation of the troops during the evacuation of Boston, receiving the thanks of the military commander General Howe, and on the arrival of the latter's brother, Admiral Howe, he took part in the capture of New York. In the information he later supplied for Ralfe's *Naval Biography*, Montagu declared that he served under Howe's immediate eye and was appointed to the post of honour. *Fowey* was the advanced ship of the squadron 'and her commander by his diligence, activity and attention to orders, obtained the friendship and esteem of his admiral'.[6] From 1777 to 1779 he served as his father's flag captain on the Newfoundland station and then distinguished himself when given command of the frigate 32-gun *Pearl* in two single-ship actions, capturing the Spanish frigate *Santa Monica*, 32-guns, in September 1779 and the French 32-gun privateer *L'Espérance* in September 1780. Montagu served the rest of the war on the American station, but was then unemployed until given command of the 74-gun *Hector* during the mobilization of 1790. On the outbreak of war with France in 1793 he went in *Hector* with Gardner's squadron to the West Indies, then served in the Channel, coming under Howe's orders on 20 December 1793. It was a creditable record of service in which he had shown both courage and an ability to take responsibility. Howe, who had forewarning of his promotion in April, seems to have been happy to receive Montagu as a flag-officer under his command and to give him a responsible detached role in the coming campaign.[7]

Howe issued his orders to Montagu on 18 April. Montagu was given six ships of the line and four frigates[8] (sufficient to deal with the convoy's escorts even if they were four of the line, four frigates and two corvettes as some reports suggested). He was to escort the East India convoy, going out with the 74-gun *Suffolk*, through the Channel and across the Bay of Biscay. They would sail in company with Howe's Channel Fleet of twenty-six of the line until Howe detached them when he took the fleet to its station off Ushant in accordance with his instructions. Montagu would then continue with the East India convoy to the latitude of Cape Finisterre after which he was to take his squadron to 'Cruize from Cape Ortugal [sic] to the Latitude of Belle Isle, on or about the Meridian of such Cape; in order to intercept a French Convoy escorted, as supposed, by some Ships of Force, and very soon expected back from North America, for different Ports on the Western Coasts [of] France; The Capture or destruction of which is deemed an object of the most urgent importance at the present time.' He was to remain on that service until 15 May unless he met with the convoy first or received credible information that it had passed to the eastward beyond further pursuit. If at the end of that time he had not received intelligence that might lead him to prolong his stay to intercept the convoy he was to take his squadron back to Torbay or Plymouth to replenish supplies so as to be in suitable condition for further service and there await further orders from Howe or the Admiralty.[9]

Montagu's task however was a perplexing one. He had no definite information of the size of the convoy's escort—both two and four of the line had been mentioned. He had no information of the convoy's probable track or destination, although from the placing of his patrol line and from what the First Lord, the Earl of Chatham, was to write to him privately on 2 June, it seems that the Admiralty expected it to be bound for Bordeaux or other Biscay ports. Above all, Montagu had no news of the departure of the convoy from America or of the date of its intended arrival in France. Reports received before he sailed indicated a delayed departure. Consul Hamilton reported on 6 March that the continued severity of the weather meant that the ships at Baltimore were still detained by the ice though he was certain the convoy must sail before the end of the month. Consul Bond wrote on 8 March that the extent of the French demand had so raised the price of produce in the ports of Virginia that some time would elapse before the requisite quantity could be furnished. At that point there were eighty-nine merchant ships preparing and the twelve warships were also taking in flour. On 11 March, Hamilton wrote that ships were now starting to come down from Baltimore, though on 30 March he reported that they were still in the Chesapeake and waiting the arrival of ships from New York and Philadelphia which were hourly expected.

Letters also dated 30 March from Virginia were carried by incoming American ships and reported in *The Times* on 30 April, which further stated the value of the convoy at £1½ million and that it was due to sail on 2 April.[10] In fact on that day Consul Hamilton wrote that two corvettes left for France with news of the proposed movement and course of the convoy. The convoy commander, Rear-Admiral Pierre Vanstabel, at last weighed anchor on 15 April but was detained by adverse winds, and it was not until 17 April that the convoy finally set sail, consisting in all of 156 sail according to Consul Hamilton who watched it leave.[11] Vanstabel left behind him a 40-gun frigate and a 16-gun brig to detain in port the 32-gun British frigate *Daedalus* in order to prevent it from carrying the news ahead of the convoy's departure. In consequence news was not received from America of the sailing of the convoy until mid-June.[12]

In the event, Howe also had difficulties in getting his convoy together and his departure was similarly delayed, so that on 2 May he gave supplementary orders to Montagu extending the latter's stay on his patrol line until 20 May, after which he was to return to the fleet rendezvous off Ushant to be employed as circumstances might then appear to require.[13] Howe finally sailed from St Helen's on 2 May and when he reached the Lizard on 4 May he detached Montagu and the convoy. Montagu escorted his charges to the latitude of Cape Finisterre where on 11 May he released the East Indiamen on their way and turned back to his cruising station between Cape Ortegal and the latitude of Belle Isle to seek the incoming French grain convoy. He was still operating very much in the dark as to its course and time of arrival, for as the Secretary of the Admiralty, Philip Stephens, confessed to Howe on 21 May when commenting on Montagu's supplementary orders, they had received no news yet that the French convoy had actually left America. Howe was directed to order Montagu back again to his station after his time had expired or to send a replacement squadron to cruise there until it encountered the convoy, or received either credible information that it had already passed or that it was not now expected to come to Europe.[14]

In fact, on 11 May, the day that Montagu left his convoy for his patrol line north of Cape Ortegal (longitude 7°52′W) between the latitudes 43°43′ and 47°21′N, the French convoy was encountered by a Dutch merchantman north-west of the Azores at latitude 40°12′N, longitude 36°22′W—still nearly three weeks away. This news was not however received until 6 June when the Dutchman was spoken to by Howe's fleet. However when Montagu's ships began their patrol he quickly discovered that he was not alone in searching for the convoy. On 15 May he intercepted the 20-gun French sloop *Le Maire Guitton* returning to Brest with ten Channel Islands' merchantmen captured from an outward-bound Newfoundland convoy. Interrogation of his prisoners revealed that the convoy had been taken on 10 May together with its escort, the frigate *Castor*, by a French squadron of five of the line and two frigates under Admiral Nielly which had left Brest on 10 April to await the convoy from America between latitudes 45° and 48°N and about two degrees eastward or westward of the longitude of Tenerife (16°40′W). Nielly had still not met with the convoy when they left him three days before.[15] It could be inferred from this that the convoy had not yet passed Montagu's patrol line and that it was imminently expected, since Nielly had been waiting for so long. However, since Nielly was to the westward of Montagu he was likely to encounter the convoy first, in which case, whether the convoy's escort was two or four of the line, the combined French force would outnumber Montagu's six battleships. He sent the frigate *Venus* back to inform Howe of what he had learned. Since he was uncertain that he could find Nielly's squadron, he decided to move his patrol line northward parallel with the station of the French admiral but he remained on his present longitude in case the news of the French strength led Howe to send him reinforcements.[16]

Howe had arrived off Brest on 5 May and, having ascertained that the French fleet was still in port, departed to cruise the Bay of Biscay in accordance with his orders until 18 May when he returned to Ushant only to find next day that the French had sailed. That same evening the *Venus* reached him from Montagu, and fearing that the latter's squadron would be sandwiched between vastly superior forces he hastened off to the south-west to support his subordinate. However, on the way on 21 May, he encountered prizes taken by the French fleet from a Dutch convoy who indicated that it was only a few leagues further to his westward and he diverted his course in pursuit. All this was unknown to Montagu, who stayed on his station waiting for Howe until 23 May when one of his frigates recaptured another Dutch prize and he was told that the French fleet was at sea with twenty-seven of the line (in fact twenty-five) and eight frigates. Confirmation of this came from other recaptures and from neutral ships in the next few days, some of whom had seen the French fleet only the day before, and he 'judged it prudent to use every possible effort to rejoin the Fleet under the command of the Earl of Howe on his cruizing station'. In fact by going back towards Ushant he was now moving away from Howe who was chasing the French fleet in the opposite direction. On his way, however, he found from further recaptures up to 27 May that Howe had been seen as far to the westward as longitude 14°W and he concluded that his commander-in-chief had received information of the sailing of the Brest fleet and had gone in pursuit of them.[17]

It remained for Montagu, alone in his first command, to decide what to do next. He seems to have considered his convoy-seeking role as over—he had remained several days longer on his station than he had been ordered by Howe and he still had no positive news of the convoy nor new orders from Howe to depart from his present instructions. He therefore did not return to his patrol line. His information of the size of the French fleet made it superior to Howe's, especially if it joined up with Nielly, but having already decided that he would not be able to find Nielly out in the Atlantic, he presumably felt that he also would not be able to find his commander-in-chief in order to reinforce him. Consequently he did not go in search of Howe. His instructions told him that when he left his patrol line he should go to the Ushant rendezvous for further orders, but since Howe clearly was not there he reverted to his fall-back orders to return to Plymouth to resupply and await fresh instructions from Howe or the

Admiralty. He told the Admiralty that he had returned to port to communicate his intelligence to the Board, replenish his squadron's topsails and yards, and land his prisoners, expecting to find orders from Howe for his future proceedings: all of which as he reiterated many years later was 'in strict compliance with the spirit of the orders received from Lord Howe'.[18]

On 31 May he reported to the Admiralty that he had arrived in Plymouth Sound that morning and had given orders to complete immediately with beer and water and be ready to proceed to sea at the shortest notice. Their Lordships replied on 2 June approving his conduct but declaring it 'of very great importance that you should return to sea as soon as possible . . .'. His squadron of six of the line and three frigates would be reinforced by four more 74s and five frigates, to which a 64-gun ship was added next day.[19] With these he was to return with the utmost expedition to Howe's rendezvous off Ushant and remain there until he received either further orders or news of Howe's whereabouts that would enable him to rejoin his commander-in-chief. If however he received any well-grounded information of the approach of Vanstabel's convoy from America and of its course, then he should make the most likely disposition of his squadron to intercept it. An accompanying private letter from the First Lord, the Earl of Chatham, explained that Ushant seemed the place where there was the best chance of rejoining Howe and, if there had been an action, of protecting any disabled ships or intercepting any of the enemy returning to Brest. Since the French fleet was out, it might be their intention that the convoy should make Ushant, but more probably it would push for Bordeaux. If Montagu received any news of it he should act accordingly since its interception was the most urgent object. His reinforcements were intended to make him superior to the combined force of its escort and Nielly if the latter's squadron had joined it, and Chatham added that all their intelligence indicated that only two ships of the line would be escorting the convoy from America.[20]

Before Montagu's new orders reached him on the morning of 4 June he learned that Howe was in contact with the French fleet. On the morning of 3 June the frigate *Pallas* arrived in Plymouth having just spoken to the 74-gun *Audacious* returning damaged

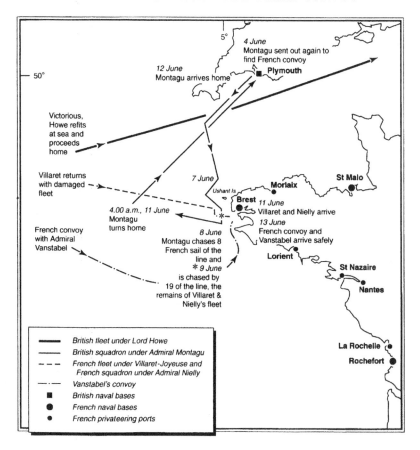

Fig. 5.i. Chart of operations, 4–12 June 1794.

from Howe's first action with Villaret on 28 May. *Audacious* herself anchored in the Sound that evening. Next day Montagu received his new orders and he sailed in the afternoon of 4 June with eight 74s and six frigates, picking up the 64 en route (see Fig. 5.i).[21] Hot on his heels followed further news and instructions from the Admiralty which had at last received news of a firm sighting of the convoy at sea—from a Bristol merchant ship, which had seen a large fleet of about 150 sail on 12 May in latitude 39°10′N, longitude 35°36′W, steering to the south-west to be out of the way of British cruisers and after to sail up into the Bay of Biscay. Montagu was now required, if there were no orders from Howe or any firm news of the whereabouts of the convoy when he reached the Ushant rendezvous, to stretch across the Bay immediately with a view to intercepting the convoy. If he received good information that it had passed beyond possibility of overtaking it, he should then return to the rendezvous to await orders from Howe or such certain intelligence of his situation as would enable him to join his commander-in-chief, which he was to endeavour to do. Since this further information and instructions did not reach Plymouth until after his departure, it is uncertain whether they ever caught up with him.[22]

Montagu arrived off Ushant on the afternoon of 8 June with eight 74-gun and one 64-gun ships of the line and three frigates in company (another frigate joined him that evening).[23] He immediately encountered a French squadron of eight of the line and four frigates which he chased 'as near to the port of Brest as prudence would permit'.[24] One of his frigates reported another 50- or 64-gun ship to windward and two ships of the line in Brest Water which confirmed him in his decision to take up station six to eight leagues WNW of Ushant, with the force in Brest to leeward, so as to enable the rest of his reinforcements to join him in safety. There he was next morning when over the horizon from the west came Villaret's fleet limping home after the actions of 28, 29 May and 1 June. There were nineteen ships of the line, three frigates and two smaller craft. Two three-deckers and two 74s were completely dismasted and another 74 considerably damaged, and these were under tow by the others—a three-decker and thirteen 80- and 74-gun ships which appeared to be in good order. As Montagu approached them, with the wind from the north, his first thought was to maintain his freedom of manoeuvre by getting to windward of them, but when the bad sailing qualities of two of his 74s, *Alexander* and *Ganges*, left them lagging astern, he decided he would not be able to weather the French fleet with his whole force and so he put about and tacked to leeward of the French. This put him between the incoming fleet and the squadron in Brest, so he edged away southward seeking to stay in a position to act against the fleet if opportunity offered but, he reported, 'they kept so closely connected and guarded with so much care their disabled ships that it was not in my power to take any step that was likely to contribute to His Majesty's Service'.

Villaret put up a bold front and for a while pursued Montagu's squadron, but any hopes Montagu might have had of luring him to leeward of his home haven[25] were ended at about 5 p.m. when Villaret hauled off towards Brest. For the next twenty-four hours Montagu ranged to the north-west in hopes of meeting Howe's pursuing fleet, but not finding his commander-in-chief, and judging that he must have reached the Channel, he bore up at 4 a.m. on 11 June and returned to Plymouth 'in order to communicate my Information and receive further Instructions from their Lordships'. He justified his termination of his cruise by explaining that with the French now concentrated in Brest 'and as their united force will be very considerable I judged the great Object of their Lordship's Orders for my cruising on the Earl Howe's Rendezvous to be at an end, or my keeping the Sea, as I have not acquired the least information respecting the American convoy'.[26]

This was the last of a series of decisions made over forty-eight hours that effectively wrecked Montagu's career, for on the evening of 12 June, as he was anchoring in Cawsand Bay outside Plymouth, Admiral Vanstabel with the American convoy was making his landfall at the Penmarchs. Vanstabel passed through the area of Howe's 29 May action with Villaret on the following day (Villaret had drawn Howe to the northward after that action) and on 2 June the convoy commander picked up one of the French casualties from the fight, the 74-gun *Montagnard* under tow from a frigate. Deciding that if the British fleet was victorious then it was likely to be waiting off the central Iroise passage into Brest, he detoured to the southward to approach that port via the treacherous southern Passage du Raz through which he passed with his convoy in the night of 12–13 June. Next day he joined Villaret's fleet that had anchored in Bertheaume Bay outside the entrance to Brest Water, and fleet and convoy passed into the harbour on 14 June.[27] It was not until 2 July that the London newspapers carried a report from Paris, dated June 20, announcing the arrival of 116 sail of the long-expected American fleet at Brest.[28]

On reaching Plymouth Montagu asked and was granted leave

to strike his flag on grounds of ill-health. He was never given another sea-going command again. Promotion came in the normal course: in June 1795 he was appointed vice admiral an in January 1801 he became a full admiral, but without employment. In 1799 he was offered the post of port admiral at the Nore, which he turned down because he wanted an active command and thought this base post beneath him. In 1800 Lord St Vincent wanted him for a command in his Channel Fleet but others were appointed in his stead. When St Vincent became First Lord of the Admiralty in the following year, Montagu applied to him for employment only to be told that 'there is an insuperable bar to your being employed in any way' which St Vincent had not been aware of and which his oath of secrecy prevented him from divulging. Montagu defended himself by sending all his letters and papers on the events of May–June 1794 to the First Lord in order to show that he had 'most punctually fulfilled every order and instruction that I received from Earl Howe, in the first instance, and the Lords Commissioners of the Admiralty in the second', and in 1803 St Vincent offered him another shore post as port admiral at Portsmouth which he accepted (he could not afford to refuse this time, moreover it was the most important base command and had been held by his father). He served at Portsmouth for five and a half years, but this was to be his final posting. In the victory celebrations at the end of the wars in 1815 he was knighted as a GCB and he died on 24 December 1829.[29]

A clue to the nature of the 'insuperable bar' to Montagu's further employment emerged when controversy broke out over the episode on the publication of the first edition of Captain Brenton's *Naval History of Great Britain* in 1823. Brenton had been a midshipman in Montagu's squadron on board *Bellona* throughout his two cruises and he had gained unique information of the French viewpoint when in 1809 he brought home Villaret, then governor of Martinique, after the capture of that colony. Brenton was highly critical of Montagu. He accused him of running for home the moment he heard the French fleet was near him in May, even though the American convoy, his object, was still at sea and to westward of him. He criticized Montagu for avoiding battle with the French fleet on 9 June when all in the British squadron anxiously expected the signal to engage and when 'many officers under similar circumstances might have so done'. In support he quoted Villaret as saying that when he saw Montagu's squadron between him and Brest he was 'petrified'. His battle-damaged vessels were in the very worst condition, their decks full of sick and wounded, and another combat was the last thing he wanted. Lastly Brenton blamed Montagu for then leaving his station and returning to Plymouth, thus letting Vanstabel's convoy into Brest.[30]

Montagu indignantly demanded that Brenton withdraw his accusations and eventually the latter agreed to withdraw his most critical remarks from subsequent editions of his book, but during the acrimonious war of words both in newspapers and in pamphlets an article appeared in the *Morning Chronicle* of 14 May 1823 that 'We have reason to believe . . . the insuperable bar to have been the late king, who, as everyone knows, was apt to take very strong dislikings, very often without good grounds, and who, when he had conceived a dislike, could not easily be brought to abandon it.' It is highly probable that George III shared Brenton's critical opinion of Montagu's conduct. His faith in the fighting powers of British seamen was such that in 1779 he was confident that the thirty-eight ships of the line of the Channel fleet could give a good account of themselves against a Franco-Spanish combined fleet of fifty, and he had been eager for an action, trusting in Divine Providence and the ardour of the officers and men of his fleet. He also believed in his admirals using their initiative, applauding when Arbuthnot rushed to the defence of Jersey in 1779 '. . . the commander that when he sees the service requires it strikes out a path different from his Instructions feeling it is at the risk of his life . . .'. The King would not have readily accepted Montagu's concern at the size of the forces opposed to him or his justification that he acted in the spirit of his instructions. By allowing both the French fleet and the American convoy to get into Brest without further damage, Montagu failed to provide the final triumphant gilding to the laurels that the King's favourite admiral, Earl Howe, had earned from his 1 June victory.[31]

In his reply to Brenton, Montagu did his best to vindicate himself. He showed that he had waited on his station for Howe's arrival for several days beyond the time in his instructions before returning to Plymouth in May. He declared that on 9 June he would certainly have attacked Villaret's ships if Howe's fleet or any part of it had been in sight, but in its absence he had eight 74s and one 64 against nineteen enemy three-deckers, 80s and 74s in compact order. If an admiral was to fight a battle under great disadvantage and disparity of force he must have some great object to obtain, but what object could Montagu have had except a personal one? He could not cherish the least hope of capturing any of Villaret's ships—he had no grounds to suspect Villaret of cowardice; Villaret was not followed by Howe's fleet so Montagu could not know how the action had terminated and the French could not be considered a beaten and flying enemy. Moreover, if any of his ships were crippled in an engagement and if the French squadron in Brest had sallied out to Villaret's assistance, then 'the whole of my little force must have been carried into a French port'. He therefore placed his squadron in a position where, if worsted, he could retreat without disgrace to his flag. On the whole, and despite the remarkable victories achieved during the ensuing wars, contemporary naval opinion and commentators would seem to have agreed with Montagu rather than Brenton and (probably) the King. Montagu himself claimed that St Vincent had told him that he 'always admired' his conduct with the French fleet, and James in his *Naval History* strongly supported Montagu against Brenton's accusations.[32]

As regards his subsequent withdrawal to Plymouth, Montagu asserted that he did so 'under the spirit of my orders' and that he was also directed by Lord Howe to do so. He further claimed that Vanstabel's convoy made Belle Isle and did not approach the track he was ordered to cruise off Brest. If he was wrong about the latter point, he was right about Howe, who must share some responsibility for the final escape of the American convoy. After his victory on 1 June, concern about his own damaged ships and the desire to protect his prizes led Howe to decide to return to port rather than pursue the French. During his homeward passage he encountered a Swedish vessel on 9 June whose master said that on 4 June he had been on board the French commander of a convoy of 104 sail bound for Brest. The convoy was then in latitude 47°50'N and longitude 13°W. Since Howe was at latitude 49°N, longitude 16°W, and the wind for several days was from the south-west, he concluded that the convoy was now well past him and into port. He therefore despatched two frigates to search out Montagu at his rendezvous and recall him to port, and one of these, the *Southampton*, made contact with Montagu as he returned to Plymouth on 12 June.[33]

It is possible therefore that Montagu would have received his orders to return to port before Vanstabel's arrival even if he had not already decided to return himself. Could he have intercepted the convoy? The chances of finding it out in the Atlantic on his first cruise were remote. He would have had to have waited on his patrol line at least another ten days beyond his 20 May recall date before the convoy arrived and even then his patrol line was so long that it might have slipped through undiscovered. Even Nielly, who stayed out longer and might be supposed to have had better information, never found the convoy and finally joined up with the Brest fleet on 30 May. Rather than search out in the wide Atlantic, it might have been better to wait off one of the principal landfalls (such as Cape Ortegal or Belle Isle) for the convoy to appear. However, deciding at which landfall to wait was likely to depend on the port to which the convoy was bound, and throughout neither Montagu nor the Admiralty had the least intelligence of which port was intended or which landfall Vanstabel would choose. If Montagu had followed Chatham's 2 June suggestion and the Admiralty's last instructions (which it is uncertain he received) of 3 June and proceeded immediately into the Bay of Biscay when he found no orders from Howe nor news of the convoy on reaching the Ushant rendezvous on 8 June, then he would probably have been too far south when the convoy made its landfall on the evening of 12 June. Had he sailed in that direction on 10 June, rather than going west in search of Howe or the convoy[34], he might indeed have run into it. However, by going west instead of south he was moving away from Vanstabel, now approaching Brest on a southern sweep. Had he simply stayed on his station, six to eight leagues WNW of Ushant, he would probably have been too far north to catch Vanstabel coming up through the Passage du Raz.

When some months later Earl Spencer replaced Chatham at the Admiralty and discussed Montagu's performance with his predecessor, they concluded that he was 'unlucky but in no shape culpable'.[35] Montagu seems to have been an ordinarily competent officer thrown into the deep end in his first operational command by being given an extraordinary task made still more difficult by the lack of information about his quarry. Already in ill health before he set off for Ushant[36], he opted to take a series of 'prudent' decisions that he could reconcile with his instructions (he always prided himself on his attention to his instructions[37]) and on each occasion the French were able to draw advantage. In consequence his first operational command was also his last.

Notes

1. PRO, ADM 2/1347, Draft of Instructions for Admiral Earl Howe, Secret, 17 April 1794.
2. This report was false but it gave rise to subsequent rumours that the convoy would be escorted back to France by four of the line, e.g. in *The Times*, 30 April 1794.
3. Five million livres or £200,000 sterling.
4. PRO, FO 5/6, Reports from Consul Bond, 20, 23 Feb., from Consul Hamilton 6, 9, 22 Jan., 11, 19 Feb. 1794.
5. PRO, ADM 2/1347, Instructions for Howe, 17 April 1794.
6. James Ralfe, *Naval Biography of Great Britain* (London, 1828) vol. 2, p. 7. This claim however should be qualified by the fact that Montagu was not among those mentioned by Howe as having distinguished themselves in any of his official dispatches reporting the capture of New York printed in the *London Gazette* in 1776.
7. Ralfe, *Naval Biography*, vol. 2, pp. 6–24; *Dictionary of National Biography*, vol. 13 (1917) pp. 694–95; National Maritime Museum, Curtis Papers (microfilm), Howe to Curtis 5, 9, 12 April 1794.
8. *Hector, Arrogant, Theseus, Ganges, Bellona, Alexander* 74s; *Pallas, Hebe, Venus, Circe* frigates.
9. PRO, ADM 1/100 ff.257–58, Instructions to Montagu 18 April (in Howe to Stephens 22 April), f. 269v McBride to Stephens 23 April, f. 320 Howe to Stephens 14 May; ADM 2/1347 Instructions to Howe 17 April 1794.
10. Sir George Montagu, *A Refutation of the Incorrect Statements and Unjust Insinuations contained in Captain Brenton's Naval History of Great Britain as far as the same refers to the conduct of Admiral Sir George Montagu G.C.B.* (London, 1823) pp. 29–30 Chatham to Montagu, 2 June; PRO, FO 5/6 Reports from Consul Bond, 8

March, from Consul Hamilton 6, 11, 30 March; ADM 1/100 McBride to Stephens 9 April, Howe to Stephens, 27 April; *The Times*, 30 April 1794.

11. The convoy was made up of 127 French and American merchant ships, the rest being warships. They carried 67,000 barrels of flour, also bacon, salt-beef and hides. The West Indiamen also contained 11,241 barrels of coffee, 7,163 barrels of sugar, as well as cotton, cocoa, rice and indigo. P. Jarnoux, 'Autour des combats de Prairal: Le convoi Van Stabel et les approvisonnements Americains en 1793–1794' in *Les marines française et britannique face aux Etats-Unis (1776–1865)* (Vincennes, Service historique de la marine, 2000) pp. 173–80). When seen by a Danish merchantman on 2 May the convoy was down to 116 merchantmen escorted by two sail of the line and eight frigates (*The Times*, 9 June 1794).

12. PRO, FO 5/6 Hamilton's reports 2, 19 April, Bond's of 29 April 1794.

13. Montagu, *Refutation*, p. 23, Secret instructions to Montagu 2 May 1794.

14. PRO, ADM 2/1347, Stephens to Howe 21 May 1794.

15. Neilly's early departure from Brest and long wait at his rendezvous would seem to indicate that the French were scarcely better informed than the British about Vanstabel's departure date. This had repercussions at the battle of the Glorious First of June when Neilly's crews were seriously weakened by sickness through having been at sea for so long.

16. PRO, ADM 1/100 ff.324–25, 329–30 Montagu's reports of 15 May; British Library Add Mss 23,207, ff.15–16. Intelligence obtained by ships of Montagu's squadron 15 May 1794.

17. PRO, ADM 1/100 ff.320, 361–361v Howe's reports 14 May, 3 June; ff. 345–47 Montagu to Stephens 29 May 1794.

18. PRO, ADM 1/100 ff.345–345v, 348–348v Montagu to Stephens 29, 30 May 1794; Montagu, *Refutation*, p. 5.

19. *Colossus, Minotaur, Swiftsure, America* 74s; *Druid, Blonde, Perseus, Eurydice, Porcupine* frigates; *Ruby* 64.

20. PRO, ADM 1/100 f. 355 Montagu's report of 31 May; ADM 2/1347 Instructions to Montagu 2 June; Montagu, *Refutation*, pp. 29–30 Chatham to Montagu, Private, 2 June 1794.

21. *The Times*, 6 June 1794 p. 3; PRO, ADM 1/100 f. 345, Montagu to Stephens 4 June; ADM 2/605 pp. 343–44. Stephens to Howe 10 June 1794. *Swiftsure* had not arrived at Plymouth from Ireland and *America* had just left for Portsmouth. Of the frigates, *Druid, Perseus* and *Eurydice* were unavailable (the first and last were in action with

a French squadron off Guernsey on 8 June) and were replaced by *Concorde* and *La Nymphe*. The 64-gun *Ruby* joined him off the Lizard. His total force consisted of *Hector, Alexander, Arrogant, Bellona, Ganges, Theseus, Minotaur, Colossus 74s, Ruby 64; Circe, Hebe, Pallas, Blonde, Concorde, La Nymphe* frigates. The *Porcupine* frigate joined off Brest in the evening of 8 June.

22. PRO, ADM 2/1347 Instructions to Montagu 3 June enclosing James Jones to Chatham 2 June from Bristol. These orders did not reach Plymouth until after Montague had sailed and there is no acknowledgement in his surviving reports of 8 and 11 June that he ever received them. However, another report from Montagu of 9 June was pocketed by Howe and is missing, and it is possible that he received these June further instructions by the frigate *Porcupine* which left Plymouth later and joined him late on 8 June.

23. E. P. Brenton, *The Naval History of Great Britain* (London, 1837) vol. 1, p. 146. The *Porcupine* frigate was the late arrival (PRO, ADM 1/100 f.379v, Montagu's report 8 June 1794).

24. This squadron had just returned to Brest from Cancale where it had been based in preparation for an attack on the Channel Islands.

25. In his justification in 1823 he declared that his purpose was to draw Villaret's fleet away from its port in the hope that some of Howe's fleet might still appear in pursuit. Montagu, *Refutation*, pp. 10–11.

26. PRO, ADM 1/100 ff.379–79v, 395–96, Montagu's reports of 8, 12 June 1794; Brenton, *Naval History*, vol. 1, pp. 146–48; W. James, *The Naval History of Great Britain* (London, 1837) vol. 1, pp. 170–72.

27. E. Chevalier, *Histoire de la Marine Française sous la Première République* (Paris, 1886) pp. 144–45. Jarnoux, 'Auteur des combats de Prairal', *Les marines française et britannique face aux Etats-Unis*, pp. 181–82. The most recent calculation gives Vanstabel's convoy on arrival as 116 merchantmen, sixteen prizes taken en route, and twelve warships. A. Delaporte, 'Combats de Prairal et Convoi de Vanstabel: le point de vue français', *Revue Historique des Armées* no. 201 (1995) p. 19 fn. 8.

28. *The Times*, 2 July 1794, p. 3.

29. Montagu, *Refutation*, pp. 40–53; Ralfe, *Naval Biography*, vol. 2, p. 14; *Dictionary of National Biography*, vol. 13, p. 695.

30. Montagu, *Refutation*, pp. 3–7, 12 quoting from Brenton, *Naval History* (London 1823) vol. 1, pp. 296–99; Brenton, *Naval History* (1837 ed.) vol. 1. pp. 145–49.

31. *Statement of a Correspondence which has taken place between Admiral Sir*

George Montagu G.C.B. and Captain Edward Pelham Brenton, subsequent to the Publication of Sir George Montagu's refutation of the incorrect statements and injurious insinuations contained in Captain Brenton's Naval History (London, 1823) pp. xiii–xvi, xx–xxi; Sir John Fortescue (ed.), *The Correspondence of King George the Third from 1760 to December 1783* (London, 1928) vol. 4, pp. 334, 380, 396–97, 406.

32. Montagu, *Refutation*, pp. 3–11; *Statement of a Correspondence* p. v; James, *Naval History*, vol. 1, pp. 178–79.

33. Montagu, *Refutation*, pp. 12–13; PRO, ADM 1/100 ff.392–93, 396 Howe to Stephens 11 June, Montagu to Stephens 12 June 1794.

34. Howe inferred from a report that Montagu sent back on the evening of 9th June and which he intercepted that Montagu left his station and ranged westward in search of the convoy as well as the British fleet. PRO, ADM 1/100 ff.392–93 Howe to Stephens 11 June 1794. This letter of 9 June, pocketed by Howe, has disappeared. Montagu did not declare himself to have been looking for the convoy as well as Howe in his report on 12 June but he did say that he had found no news of its whereabouts (ibid. ff.395–96).

35. Montagu, *Refutation*, pp. 54–55. Brenton, *Naval History* (1837 edn), vol. 1, p. 149, asserted that at one point the frigate *Flora* had both the convoy and Montagu's squadron in sight but its signals were too distant to be seen or understood or if seen were not repeated. However, the Captain's log of *Flora* shows that it did not sail from Cowes until 10 June and on 11 June it was at Portland where it heard of the battle of 1 June from the damaged *Brunswick*. It was in no position to see the convoy and Montagu. The story almost certainly relates to a later incident on 25 June when *Flora* with a frigate squadron ran into the move of 42 of the convoy from Brest to Bordeaux (probably mostly St Domingo ships returning to their home port) escorted by two of the line and five frigates. The escort kept away the British warships. (PRO, ADM 51/1152 Log of the Flora 8 Jan.–12 Sept. 1794; *The Times* 7, 14 July 1794).

36. He had informed Chatham of his ill health on his return from his first cruise—see Chatham to Montagu, 2 June in Montagu, *Refutation*, p. 30.

37. See his comments on his service under Howe in 1776 in Ralfe, *Naval Biography*, vol. 2, p. 7, and in May–June 1794 in Montagu, *Refutation*, pp. 5, 12, 47.

6

The Convoy, the Grain and their Influence on the French Revolution

Lawrence Evans

Captain Mahan's account of the Battle of the Glorious First of June clearly demonstrates why he was so influential among such a wide audience: among professional navy men and intellectual laymen, among policy makers from congressmen to the Kaiser. He was, of course, a thorough professional; he himself had made the transition from sail to steam and from the broadside to the turret gun. In short he was a master of his subject.

In writing, his style is clear and uncluttered with technical jargon. He gives a concise and vivid description of the damage done to the French navy by the Revolution and a measured evaluation of the effect on the French fighting ability. He parallels this by an evaluation of the Royal Navy. He addresses the great improvements to the fleet since the American war and the arrival at the top of the commanders of the navy of that group of outstanding captains and admirals that drove the French from the sea and crushed Napoleon's hope of eliminating the last barrier to his ambition. We are provided with an overview of the dispositions and actions of the two navies, their strategic assumptions and their respective roles of the sea in the war. The actual combat is given clearly and the progress of the battle from the opening gun to the withdrawal of the two fleets from the scene of the action. Who won the battle? Mahan's assessment was that in a way both sides did. The Royal Navy sank or captured several French warships and the French got the convoy through. But one might say with equal truth that both sides lost the battle. Either way, that is mere score keeping.

A battle is not an end unto itself. The real question is did the battle improve or impair the war-making power of the state; was the ability of France to fight England improved by the success of the convoy more than it was harmed by the loss of several valuable war vessels? In other words, what was the influence of the Battle of the Glorious First of June on the French Revolution? The answer to that question depends on the state of the grain supply. Certainly the French armada was willing to pay a high price and take great risks for that grain.

Before we proceed to consider the state of the grain supply, an important fact must be noted. France was normally sufficient in grain and the convoy represented an extraordinary effort on the part of the French government. The convoy was not a segment of a bridge of boats bringing essential supplies and the attack did not represent a threat to the French government policies as the attack on the Atlantic convoys did to British policy in the two world wars of the twentieth century.

After considering this circumstance, the perceptive observer will note that a population of 25,000,000 people eats at least 3,000,000 tons of grain every year and wonder again why Robespierre placed such a high value on a supply of grain that would make little difference to the nation. Then the observer would have to take into account the fact that transportation in France was extremely expensive and from Brittany to Paris, the focus of the problem, the whole load could be consumed just carrying it that distance. Given the problem was in Paris, the logical object of the shipments would be the Channel Ports.

It is clear that the confused and contradictory state of the grain supply in 1793 and 1794 cannot produce the basis for an intelligent understanding of the affair of the convoy and its effect on the French Revolution or the policies of the French government. For that perspective we must consider how and why the crisis facing France developed. Until the nineteenth century, France was a society based on what was essentially, in modern terms, subsistence agriculture. Most of the population was engaged in producing food; most of the population, over seventy per cent, depended for most of their diet, from seventy to ninety per cent of the calorie intake, on grain. The surplus left to feed the non-agricultural population provided only a narrow margin of security for the food supply of the towns and cities. With an urban population of ten per cent, a drop of five per cent in the harvest, not uncommon, would in fact cut the grain surplus available for the cities by fifty per cent.

On the average, France grew enough grain to feed its people in normal years with a substantial surplus, but it had only enough storage capacity, about one year's production, to tide the country over one bad harvest, and two successive poor years would cause substantial want and even starvation for the most unfortunate. This was the average, but many regions did not reach this average. France had several agricultural regions, distinguished by climate and physical conditions, and each with its own problems and advantages. Some produced two, three, or four times their own grain requirements, others less than a half; some concentrated on grain, others on wine and imported their grain; some, in the Mediterranean regions, left half their land fallow; others, in the north, left a third; some, in the Midi for example, grew just about enough grain in good years but, because of poor communications, could suffer actual famine in a bad year when their neighbours were undergoing a mere shortage and high prices, because of the physical barriers to the transport of relief supplies.[1] In general, grain production in France seems to have reached its maximum in the eighteenth century, both in terms of production per unit and the area under cultivation, while at the same time population increased by about twenty to twenty-five per cent, from about twenty million to twenty-six, give or take a million or so. The impact of these circumstances was felt with different intensities in different regions of France, but for everyone the margin was getting narrower and narrower, and the impact of pessimistic projections of next year's harvest or of major changes in patterns of grain purchases, or any other evidence that grain might be short next year, had every year it seems a more profound and damaging affect on market supplies and prices.

The outbreak of war in 1792 and the second revolution culminating in the rising of August 10 absorbed much of the energy of the activists of all parties. But while the harvest of that year was more than adequate in terms of normal levels of supply and demand, the requirements of the Army, the loss of manpower to the volunteer movement, the depreciated *assignats* (paper currency), and high prices generally meant continued high prices for grain.[2] The situation in Paris was particularly bad throughout the winter of 1792 to 1793 and popular demonstrations were frequent; in February the most radical sections of the City demanded a maximum price for bread. By the end of March the supply had failed and mobs ransacked bakers' shops. The uncertain future, the breakdown of traditional authority, and the depreciated paper currency meant that producers on all levels held on to their grain; the grain that did come on the market had to pass the gauntlet of local officials and the demands of the producing region before it could be sent up to Paris. And all the time high prices matched low supplies cutting the real income of townspeople, and *Parisiens* in particular, by a half and more.

On 4 May the Convention passed the first Law of the Maximum.[3] This plan might have worked had it not been that the value of paper money dropped steadily, and had not the new maximum price reinforced the reluctance of producers to part with their grain. As a result, the Paris markets were deserted and Paris suffered even more. Once again the government responded by passing a law adding a new category of monopolists, those who kept from public sale any goods 'of the first necessity', who did not place them on the market daily and who permitted such goods to deteriorate in storage.[4] On 9 August, the Government declared that all goods of necessity were public property since they were produced from the land of *La Patrie*, and established public granaries in each district of Paris.[5] The movement to re-establish a controlled grain trade culminated in the new Law of the Maximum of 11 September 1793. This set wheat prices for all of France at fourteen *livres* a quintal, later raised by one *livre* to cover transport. Maximum prices for other necessities and official wage scales were set by the Law of 29 September. In addition to setting prices, the Laws of the Maximum required all farmers, proprietors and other holders of supplies to declare all the grains in their possession on pain of confiscation.[6]

The new Law of the Maximum merely guaranteed that almost

no domestic grain would be sent to public markets. Moreover, the law was so rigid that many millers and merchants were prosecuted for moving and selling grains in the normal course of business and many others were denounced by their neighbours out of animosity and spite. As a result, there was wholesale evasion of the law with the active assistance of local officials, and even those who were caught and prosecuted often faced court proceedings conducted by their own relatives and friends. Underlying all the confusion and distress brought about by the new laws was the universal official price of grain, which totally ignored the great variations in production and transportation costs from area to area, even in normal times; the consequences of this anomaly spread through the entire economy and had important effects on wages paid to farm workers, which varied from village to village, and created a great reservoir of dissatisfaction and resentment against the authorities.[7]

The demands made on the food supply by the army put the seal on the breakdown of the food supply. The requisition of horses and wagons and the loss of manpower to the army reduced significantly the crop harvested. Furthermore, the huge requirements of grain and fodder imposed on the countryside to feed the hundreds of thousands of soldiers in the revolutionary armies imposed intolerable burdens on the agricultural sectors of the economy and society, that is to say the great majority of Frenchmen. These burdens were compounded by the stupidity and ignorance of officials. Paris and its inhabitants, far more than the army, drew upon themselves the curses of the peasants as they were perceived more and more as the controlling element of the government, particularly after the fall of the Gironde and the rise to power of the Jacobins.

The Jacobin philosophy that all goods of necessity were public property and at the disposal of the government reached its logical development in 1793–94. The Government controlled the grain supply from the fields to the mouths of the consumer, and the guillotine was the ultimate sanction. The harvest was conducted under the eyes of soldiers stationed in the fields, the grain was distributed by the communes and municipalities, ground in mills run by the government, baked in communal ovens, and sold under a strict rationing system.[8] At least this was government policy. The reality was the creation of a vast illegal market based on cash and the repudiation of the *assignats*, and the rapid transfer of support for the Jacobins to the hard core of the *sans-culottes* (labouring class) of Paris.[9]

Part of the problem facing the French government lay within the nature of transport at the time. As a whole, eighteenth-century transportation was extremely expensive, not only in the consumption of food but also in cash. Land transport was the most expensive. Experiments made in Britain during the first canal building boom in the eighteenth century developed some revealing figures on relative efficiency of various means of transport measured by the capacity of a single horse: pack-horse, 275 lbs; stage wagon, 1,350 lbs, but on a macadam road, 2 tons; wagon on iron rails, 8 tons; barge on a still river, 30 tons; barge on a canal, 50 tons.[10]

Eighteenth-century France had the most highly developed land transportation system in Europe. By the end of the Napoleonic Wars there were about 8,500 leagues of Royal highways, about half in poor condition; 9,500 leagues of provincial roads in various states of disrepair; and 10,000 leagues of local and communal roads almost all of which were uniformly bad. The kingdom had good potential natural water transport, but it was undeveloped. There were four major river basins, the Seine, Loire, Rhône and Garonne. By 1789, the Seine and the Loire, and the Rhône and the Garonne were connected by canals, with the Loire-Rhône connection and the Seine-Rhône connection under construction and due to be completed in a few years. There were 121 developed navigable rivers of a total length of 2,000 leagues and 900 leagues of canals including those under construction and planned.[11] The rivers themselves varied in usefulness as arteries of communication from the raging torrent of the Rhône in the spring and fall to the usually placid waters of the Seine and its tributaries. The Rhône had decent conditions for only three months. For four months it was impassable; for six weeks there were floods when the current might reach ten or twelve miles an hour and the tow-path would in any case be submerged; and for two months or more the river would be too low to float the barges. For five months the barges made their way with reduced loadings according to the depth of the river.[12] Navigation on the

Loire was little better though conditions were not as extreme as those of the Rhône. There was drought in the summer and floods in the spring, and often ice after a bad winter. Traffic usually stopped from July to October.[13] The Seine was navigable for most of the year, at least in one direction. In former days the river was tidal for much of the distance from the sea to Paris, and vessels could move with the tide up and down stream except in the spring floods when traffic ran only down to the sea. These conditions were also to some degree characteristic of the tributaries such as the Oise and the Marne.[14] The Garonne was also tidal but the estuary was difficult to navigate; the traffic was very small and little used for the shipment of food.

Transportation by road in France was expensive, slow and uncertain. The only good roads were the principal Royal Highways, but they had been built for strategic purposes, not economic; the rest ranged from mediocre to impossible.[15] In 1770 (and under Napoleon) it took thirty days by freight wagon to travel from Paris to Marseilles, at a daily distance of twenty miles (thirty-two kilometres). The cost per 100 kilos was 13.50 francs Paris–Marseilles and 19.50 the return journey, about half British costs; this was raised to 21 and 25 francs in 1785. Even in 1825, after major work on the road system had been conducted, it took twenty-five days at a cost of 14.5 and 18 francs.[16] Between Lyons and Marseilles freight wagons running in competition with the river barges took ten days at a charge of 80 francs a ton, and when the Rhône was impassable rates were higher.[17] Through the eighteenth century, a common sight along the highways was overturned and stranded wagons. Thievery was rife. Those goods that did arrive at their destination often did so damaged by weather or rough handling.

Inland water transport in France was calculated to cost about half or a third of land transport; it was also more certain, but on many river systems, the Rhône and the Loire for instance, no traffic was carried for a third of the year or more. Time was more uncertain by river than by land and depended on the state of the river. The journey from Lyons to Arles might take three days travelling with the current at six or eight miles an hour, and over twenty days the other way; when the river was slack it could take a week with the current and two or even three months against it.

On the average a barge would make eight round trips a year from Arles to Lyons.[18] The journey from Nantes to Paris via Orléans took three weeks as a rule. With a good west wind and enough water under the keel a barge took a week or eight days to haul against the current from Nantes to the Canal d'Orléans, two days to transfer the cargo to the special barges for the journey up the Orléans canal, then ten days to Paris via the Loire and the Seine; the return trip took two weeks. If conditions were unfavourable the journey to Paris could take six weeks to two months.[19] Even after the canals from the Seine system to the Rhône were completed and barges could travel from Le Havre to Marseilles direct, it still took over a month for the journey and many shippers preferred to use the sea routes even though it might take up to three months.[20]

Sea transport, as a whole, was not a major factor in the internal trade of France.[21] Geology and meteorology had combined to make French coastal shipping expensive and uncertain in the days of sail; harbours were few and difficult to access, and in the Channel the tides and prevailing winds often made westerly passages impossible for weeks on end. The most glaring deficiency was in secure anchorages; there are no French equivalents of the Downs, the Solent, Torbay or Falmouth, where ocean-going vessels and even entire fleets may wait indefinitely for a fair wind. Anchorages for coastal vessels were even more deficient. From Jutland to Brest the only comparable facilities are the Scheldt to Antwerp and the mouths of the Rhine. The ports, though reasonably secure once a vessel was inside the constructed facilities, were significantly inferior to British ports in access and in anchorages.

Low-cost bulk cargoes such as grain were not economically viable. The French economy could not absorb the costs of high freight rates, inadequate insurance facilities (a growing factor in any efficient shipping industry and one brought to a high level in Britain), and the most important of all, uncertainty due to the destruction and capture of vessels during wartime—and from time to time the cessation of shipping together. Not only deep sea shipping, but also cabotage (or coastal shipping) was affected by these conditions until after the Napoleonic Wars. Only in the Mediterranean did French maritime trade maintain any degree of vigour at the time of the Revolution, and this activity included only the most limited internal traffic.

Traffic in the Channel was particularly vulnerable in time of war and the normal trade from the Baltic that had been an important supplement to French grain production essentially ceased when the enemy was Britain. The French navy was unable to protect sea traffic in the Channel. The same obstacles that limited commercial traffic limited the effectiveness of the French navy, compared to the Royal Navy. The French navy had no such amenity as the Solent in which to assemble and organize a fleet, where it could wait indefinitely and safely for an opportune circumstance to attack the British fleet or blockade a British port. Nor did the French have safe havens such as Torbay or Falmouth to which they might withdraw temporarily under stress of weather. A French fleet entering the Channel could never be sure that it could get out again except by the route of the Armadas and for the same reasons that drove the Spanish around the north of Scotland. In other words, the British could maintain a naval presence in the Channel and off the Atlantic coast of France while France could mount what amounted to intermittent patrols off her own coast and none at all off the British coast.

The grain fleet from North America sent to relieve the dearth of 1794, which the British fleet failed to intercept in the battle of the Glorious First of June, was headed for Brest on the Brittany coast, though the ultimate destination of the grain was Paris; shipment via Rouen and Le Havre, the natural ports for Paris, was impossible. When the grain reached Brest, it had reached only the fringes of France and still had to be transported to the consumers at a greater cost than that of shipping it across the Atlantic, and with a substantial proportion of the grain consumed in the process.[22] Despite this, it was a cost that the French government was willing to pay in addition to the price they paid in ships and lives lost to the battle itself. Paris needed the grain. Certainly had the convoy not made it to Brest, the grain would not have made it to Paris, and the hardship of the dearth would have continued. Would the effects of the loss of the grain have been great enough to have made a clearly discernable impact upon the war effort? There is no question that the government would have been facing a weakening of its position had they been unable to add the American grain to their own unsteady supply. France was volatile and Paris remained a veritable powder keg. The loss of the grain would have represented the loss of one of the most valuable commodities in the world of eighteenth-century transport, that of food. Yet France as a whole had not yet truly come to grips with the issue of distribution. None of the governments that ruled the French during the Revolution, the Girondins, the Jacobins, not the Directory, not even Napoleon, were any closer to a solution of the food supply than the Bourbons were.[23] Without such a solution, the convoy represented little more than a stop-gap method to feed Paris. In the end, it succeeded in this, but one convoy full of grain was not enough to strengthen the troubled French government. Paris was fed, the army went on to reoccupy Belgium, but Robespierre fell and France went on to struggle with the logistics of feeding its population through the changes of government that followed.

Notes

1. For a concise account of French agricultural regionalism see A.N. Duckham and G.B. Masefield, *Farming Systems of the World* (London, 1970), ch 2.6, pp. 260ff.
2. L. Sangier, *La Crise du Ble à Arras à la fin du XVIIIe Siècle 1748–1796* (Fontenoy le Comte, 1943), pp. 52–53.
3. Ibid., pp. 53–54.
4. Ibid., p. 54.
5. Ibid.
6. Ibid.
7. Ibid., pp. 67ff.
8. Ibid., pp. 108–21, 127–28.
9. Ibid., pp. 141–44.
10. L.T.C. Rolt, *Navigable Waterways* (Harlow, 1969) p. 1. There is no parallel in the French literature to the detailed and all-inclusive studies of British transportation; the fascination that railways and canals have for British professional and amateur historians has deep roots. Typically Pierre Goubert, for instance, cites no references in the section in his *Les Français et l'Ancien Régime* (2 vols, Paris, 1984) that deals with the importance of transportation. There is a comprehensive bibliography of governmental and other primary

sources and secondary works on French canals in H. Grosskreutz, *Privatkapital und kanalbau in Frankreich 1814–1848* (Berlin, 1977). *For the American experience see G.R. Taylor, The Transportation Revolution* (New York, 1951), p. 132. For a detailed historical analysis of the role of transportation in the development of an entire coalfield, see John Langton, *Geographical Change and Industrial Revolution: Coalmining in South West Lancashire, 1590–1799* (Cambridge, 1979).

11. For a contemporary account of the French transport system in the pre-railroad era, see Michel Chevalier, *Les intérêts matériels en France: travaux publics, routes, canaux, chemins de fer* (Paris, 1838); *for a brief account see* P. Chaunu et R. Gascon, *L'état et la ville. I: Histoire economique et social de la France* (Paris, 1971), pp. 379ff.

12. Felix Rivet, *La navigation à vapeur sur la Saône et le Rhône, 1783–1863* (Paris, 1962).

13. H. Pinsseau, *Histoire de la construction de l'administration et de l'exploitation du canal d'Orléans de 1676 à 1954* (Paris, 1963).

14. Cf. J. Meuvret, *Études d'histoire économique: receuil d'articles* (Paris, 1971), *passim*, and A.P. Usher, *The History of the Grain Trade in France, 1400–1710* (Cambridge, MA, 1913), pp. 71ff.

15. Chevalier, *Les intérôts matériels*.

16. Rivet, *La navigation à vapeur*, p. 42.

17. Ibid., pp. 24–25.

18. Ibid., p. 29.

19. Pinsseau, *Histoire de la construction*, pp. 147–48.

20. Chevalier, *Les intérêts matériels, pp. 62–63*.

21. Cf. P.J. Charliat, *Trois siècles d'économie maritime Française* (Paris, 1931); *also,* E. Daubigny, *Choiseul et la France d'outremer après le traité de Paris: étude sur la politique coloniale au XVIIIe siècle* (Paris, 1889).

22. On the naval operations during the Revolutionary period, see A.T. Mahan, *The Influence of Sea Power upon the French Revolution and Empire, 1793–1812* (2 vols, Boston, 1898).

23. Evans, 'The Sea, Logistics and the State: An Essay in Maritime History' (unpublished mss, 1993). This was Dr Evans' last manuscript. It is a reassessment of economic conditions and economic development in the pre-industrial world of the eighteenth century as it moved through the Industrial Revolution into modern industrial society. The three most advanced economic societies, China, France and Britain, are examined through their trade and transport of grain. This examination is supplemented by

briefer treatments of classical Rome, supplied entirely by sea, and eighteenth-century Madrid, supplied entirely by land, to give the parameters for the subject matter. The present essay has also been published, with small editorial differences, in *The Northern Mariner* vol. 5 (1995) no. 1, pp. 45–51.

7

The Glorious First of June
A Battle of Art and Theatre

Pieter van der Merwe

Our line was form'd, the French lay to,
One Sigh I gave to Poll on shore,
Too cold I thought our last Adieu—
Our parting kisses seem'd too few,
 If we should meet no more.
But love, avast! My heart is oak
Howe's daring Signal floats on high;
I see through roaring cannon's smoke—
Their Awful line subdued and broke
 They strike, they sink, they fly.
Now (danger past) we'll drink and Joke,
Sing 'Rule Britannia'; 'Hearts of Oak!'
And Toast before each Martial tune—
Howe and the Glorious first of June.[1]

Two hundred years after the event, and through the post-Nelsonic haze which indelibly tints our view of the French Wars, it is effectively impossible to re-evoke the level of public excitement that greeted Howe's victory of 1 June 1794.

In reviewing some aspects of the artistic celebration of the battle there are a few basic facts worth remembering. First, Howe's failure to achieve his ostensible aim of stopping Vanstabel aside, the action was in operational terms a decisive victory fought uniquely far from land and as a consequence of an unusually complex set of circumstances. Secondly, as the first action of a naval war its very decisiveness was also unusual; one has to go as far back as the Battle of Lowestoft in 1665 to find a similar inaugural success. The messy debacle of Ushant in 1778 or, worse, Byng at Minorca in 1756 are more characteristic of opening fleet set-pieces of previous eighteenth-century conflicts. The reasons for Howe's break with this dismal tradition are various but in public terms the response was correspondingly ecstatic. In 1794 the Navy had yet to build the myth of Nelsonic invincibility it enjoyed by the time of Trafalgar.

In looking at the public reactions, it is perhaps also of significance that it was the first naval victory of a war against a 'modern ideological enemy'; that is, one ruthlessly operating an extreme, secular political theory. This is a simplification but the British perception of early revolutionary France as what we would now call a 'terrorist state' presumably added something to a sequence of anxiety, hope, relief and celebration which surrounded the events of 28 May to 1 June 1794. The battle remains the only one after which the monarch personally visited the fleet to bestow honours and rewards, and the first for which official naval medals were struck, to be subsequently reissued in the same pattern for ensuing fleet actions.[2] Uniquely for the time, there were seven flag-officers involved and the rewards were commensurate.

The Glorious First also manifested an unprecedented level of response in pictorial and exhibition terms. A cursory tally from the National Maritime Museum's annotated catalogue of the Cust Collection of naval prints shows that English engravings of the fleet actions of the American War, issued within ten years of the event (and most within five), are all in single figures: one for Ushant, seven for Rodney's Moonlight Action, six for the Dogger Bank and eight for the Saints. Judged by numbers of published images the great naval event of that war was the defence of Gibraltar, 1782, with fifteen prints. The Glorious First produced at least thirty-three prints. By further contrast, St Vincent saw seventeen and Camperdown nineteen. These figures are far from absolute but their comparative magnitudes reasonably reflect public interest in the victory set against those which preceded and followed. It is only with the Nile—thirty-two prints—that the trade reflects a similar level of excitement.[3]

Prints were, it is to be emphasized, the prime popular commercial art of the day. In terms of steady income there was more to be gained from publishers' commissions than selling paintings to individuals, which was comparatively difficult on a practical level and itself best pursued through a reputation based on prints. If painters were themselves engravers or publishers they stood to gain both ways. Robert Dodd is a classic example who engraved his own work on a large scale: by contrast Nicholas Pocock, though not personally an engraver like Dodd, himself occasionally published fine plates of his own work, as well as supplying other publishers.

It is to Pocock that we shall turn first, then to some of the large prints of the action, and the original paintings and circumstances relating to them; finally, to related reflections of the Glorious First in panoramic entertainment and theatre.

Not least among the unique distinctions of this battle is that a professional artist recorded it in person—the first time, as far as I am aware, that a British painter deliberately embarked in the expectation of action (combatant amateurs excepted), and the first instance of a naval 'war artist' role of any sort since the days of the van de Veldes. Nicholas Pocock (1740–1821) had been a Bristol sea-captain and artistic amateur, who swallowed the anchor about 1776 and turned to full-time marine painting.[4] He was encouraged by Sir Joshua Reynolds and, from 1782, moved to London and built up a successful practice, largely among a naval clientele and in related publication. He had a high-level entrée amid the American War generation (Lord Hood was an early patron) and his success was based not only on his marine and geographical knowledge and artistic skill, but also on his social address. No one else except the Gascon émigré, or rather ex-prisoner-of-war, Dominic Serres, could boast such a combination and Serres' death in 1793 left Pocock at the head of his profession throughout the 1793–1815 conflict and beyond.[5]

How he managed to get a supercargo's berth on board one of Howe's repeating frigates, the 28-gun *Pegasus*, Captain Robert Barlow, is unknown but it must have been by a personal connection. The results include a remarkable first-hand written account

Fig. 7.i. Fog of war: *The British 74,* Invincible, *raking* La Juste. *One of Pocock's on-the-spot sketches from the* Pegasus. *NMM PAD8697.*

Fig. 7.ii. Sea of desolation: *The aftermath of the battle as witnessed by Pocock, with the* Queen Charlotte *and the* Queen *both substantially dismasted, centre left and right. NMM PAD8703.*

of the action by Pocock himself and another written by the second lieutenant of the *Brunswick*, which he carefully preserved along with four of his own battle plans (see Figs 4.i–iv in Chapter 4) and, separately, some of the most evocative watercolour studies of the reality of war under sail (see Figs 7.i–ii).[6] Pocock also painted three publicly exhibited oil pictures, of which the most important example and an even better later commission of 1811 (Fig. 7.iii) are at Greenwich, and issued several prints.[7] These include two large plates (see Fig. 7.iv) which he published himself and five of the many illustrations he later did for the monthly *Naval Chronicle*, which was to all intents the Navy's trade journal over the years of its existence, 1799–1818.[8]

At this period, prints of a notable event were issued in three ways: earliest came those which were rapidly produced in periodicals, often including simple schematic battle plans; secondly, those which were issued speculatively based on low-cost original artwork (which included the output of most 'hack' marine painters); lastly came those for which subscriptions were raised in advance by showmen or publishers who engaged painters to produce works which were themselves exhibited, sometimes for paying entry, sometimes free as part of the general promotion of a printseller's business and to raise the wind for the specific subscription issue. At this point the rapidly expanding worlds of art, related commerce and public entertainment combined.

The earliest print of the Battle of The First of June appeared within three weeks as a small plate in the *Register of the Times* of 21 June, after a drawing by William Anderson. Given the short time available, its fully finished nature is suspicious and it may in fact be a recycled image, a fairly common sort of imposition in the 'commemoratives' trade.[9] Howe's *Gazette* report had been published on 10 June; the fleet returned on 13 June and a very schematic plan of the order of battle was also published in the *Morning Herald* of 28 June.[10]

In September the map and print-seller John Fairburn issued the earliest good aquatint and line plate by William Elmes, a speculative item by his in-house marine specialist, and on 1 November two aquatints were published after Thomas Luny.[11] This is interesting because, though to all visual purposes a pair,

Fig. 7.iii. The dismasted Defence engaged with an unidentified French ship, left, and L'Achille, right. Painted by Pocock in 1811 for her pious captain (later Admiral) James Gambier. His friend Captain Pakenham of the Invincible later memorably hailed: 'Jemmy, whom the Lord loveth He chasteneth'. NMM BHC0474, Greenwich Hospital Collection.

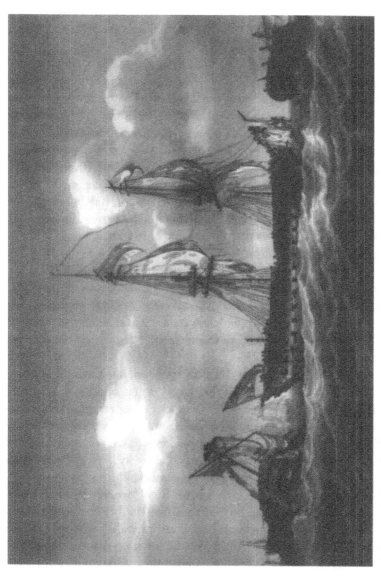

Fig. 7.iv. The second of Pocock's large aquatints, showing the Brunswick after disengaging from the sinking Vengeur (astern) and L'Achille. NMM PAH7866; the original drawing for this is also at Greenwich.

they were issued by separate publishers. Luny (a talented and prolific marine artist) gave up exhibiting paintings when war broke out in 1793, but continued working in London until (for health reasons) he moved to Teignmouth in 1807, after which he produced over 2,200 oil pictures, usually at five to ten guinea prices, until his death in 1837.

The other item of note published in 1794 is the Portsmouth publisher R. Livesay's issue of an accurate and well-annotated track chart of the action (see Fig. 7.v). The original was supplied by James Bowen, master of Howe's flagship the *Queen Charlotte* and one of the heroes of the day for his handling of her against the *Montagne*. A splendid eccentric, his reward was a commission, appointment as the Fleet's prize agent, and an eventual rise to flag rank. This item is perhaps a unique example of an authoritative eighteenth-century printed battle chart. Some similar items exist for Trafalgar but not of this large scale, specificity or provenance. It is very big (64 x 79 cm / 25 x 35 in image size) and finely done.[12]

During the course of 1794, Robert Dodd (1748–1815), the most prolific of the marine hacks of the American and French war period, and the only one who covered both from beginning to end, painted two oils which were issued as aquatints in January 1795.[13] However, his most interesting legacy of the action was the huge painting (194 x 340.5 cm / 76 x 134 in) which he completed in 1795 for the dining room of his local 'pub', The Half Way House (later the George) in London's Commercial Road (see Fig. 7.vi). In fact it is so large it was reportedly done *in situ*. It accurately shows the sinking of the *Vengeur*, going over on her beam-ends and the rescue of her crew, a recurring theme in both pictures and written accounts. Had it been done for a major collection its size would not be remarkable but it is a very rare survival of a public painting done for a low- rather than high-life situation. Its nautical appeal in a seamen's area of London, and a fair degree of technical accuracy, are probably why it survived in the pub, demolished in 1833, and in its replacement until that too was demolished in 1932. It is now at Greenwich.[14]

A further eight large battle prints were issued before July 1796, two of these being Pocock's fine *Brunswick* and *Vengeur* pair, and two others being published in Portsmouth rather than

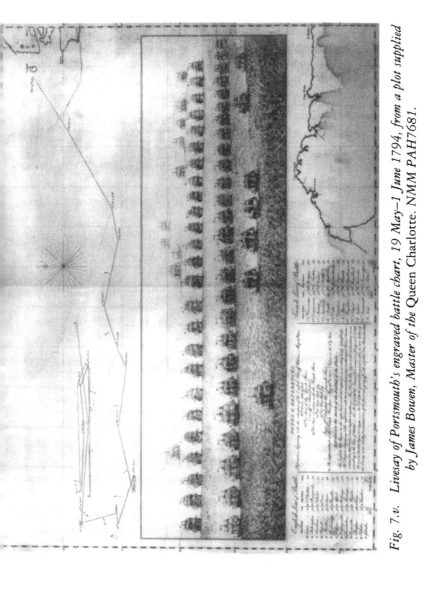

Fig. 7.v. Livesay of Portsmouth's engraved battle chart, 19 May–1 June 1794, from a plot supplied by James Bowen, Master of the Queen Charlotte. *NMM PAH7681.*

London, celebrating Hood and the *Royal George*'s part in the action.[15] A further set of six aquatints of the six French ships captured, was also issued by Livesay at Portsmouth: *La Juste* and *Sans Pareil* (both 80s), *L'America, L'Achille, Le Northumberland*, and *L'Impétueux*, all 74s.

Of all these there are only three and one other of 1799 to be considered further here. All relate to paintings first exhibited publicly as great set-pieces and for which subscriptions were raised for expensive prints.

The idea of painting large canvases for specific exhibition as a public spectacle, rather than as part of a more general artistic show, was an invention of the American-born portraitist and historical painter John Singleton Copley (1737–1815) who settled in London in 1775.[16] He launched it in spectacular way in 1781 with his exhibition of the *Death of Chatham* (Pitt the Elder, by a stroke in the House of Lords in 1778) shown in the Great Rooms at Spring Gardens. In six weeks it drew 20,000 people at a shilling a head and, with sales of the print, made him £5,000. It was also said to have made him five thousand enemies because it was done in competition with the annual Royal Academy show, reducing their attendance by a third and their gate receipts by £1,000. This was in a year when the Academy showed seven works by Gainsborough, fifteen by Reynolds and had confidently expected Copley's painting too. He was, after all, a full Academician at the time and his money-grubbing desertion to showbusiness was regarded as an insult. Copley did the same with other historical pictures, upping the odds and the profits in 1782 with his vast (5.4 m x 7.5 m / 18 x 25ft) *Destruction of the Spanish Floating Batteries at Gibraltar 1782*.[17] He of course also painted fine conventional portraits. That of Lord Howe, which was originally part of his Gibraltar presentation and is now at Greenwich, is among them (see Fig. 3.i).[18]

Copley's success as a showman was not lost on others, among them Mather Brown (1761–1831), like Copley both an American immigrant and similarly a protégé of the American-born second President of the Royal Academy, Sir Benjamin West. From 1792 to about 1797 Brown formed a partnership with the painter, engraver and print-seller Daniel Orme, to exhibit large history paintings as a loss-leader for the sale of subscription prints of

Fig. 7.vi. Robert Dodd's huge 'pub' painting of the end of the Battle of 1 June 1794. Beyond the sinking Vengeur the British Alfred is shown hove-to, with the mast of the cutter Rattler astern, rescuing the French crew. NMM BHC0469.

Fig. 7.vii. The print from Mather Brown's oil painting of Lord Howe on the quarter deck of the Queen Charlotte on 1 June 1794. It has minor differences from the large exhibited oil but records the edge detail now lost from the original (also in the NMM); for example, the figure of Captain Sir Roger Curtis, far left, is here complete. It would seem that artistic license created a more glamorous picture of Howe than the reality. A sailor who was with him was later recorded as saying that he 'was dressed during the action like a sailor in a blue jacket and fur cap, and . . . when the action was over Lord Howe was in appearance like a chimney sweep with gunpowder.' (Oliver Warner, 'Howe at the Glorious First of June', The Mariner's Mirror, 56 (1970), 2). NMM PAH 7879.

Fig. 7.viii. Lord Howe's action, or the Glorious First of June *completed in 1795 by Philippe-Jacques de Loutherbourg (1740–1812). One of the finest and largest of 18th-century battle paintings, this shows de Loutherbourg's abilities as a draftsman and colourist as well as the theatrical skills of composition for which he was celebrated; the* Queen Charlotte, *on the left, loses her foretopmast and Villaret's* Montagne, *right, pulls ahead. NMM BHC0470, Greenwich Hospital Collection.*

them. His picture of Lord Howe on the quarter-deck of the *Queen Charlotte* with the affecting death of the 'amiable' Captain Neville of the Queen's Regiment, was one of these (see Fig. 7.vii).[19]

Brown had himself visited the *Queen Charlotte* at Portsmouth and did individual portraits of all those involved. The picture was advertised as one of both nautical accuracy and 'entirely novel' through being the first naval and portrait subject for this type of exhibition. Despite its stagey appearance to a modern eye (and Brown's other work for Boydell's Shakespeare Gallery accounts for that) it gained both the approval of the King and Queen, to whom it was presented privately, of the officers shown, and of the public who came to see it in large numbers. It was exhibited— apparently without charge—in Orme's premises at 14 Old Bond Street, from January to April 1795. Orme's large print (43 x 58 cm / 17 x 22¾ in) for which it was raising the wind was issued on 1 October 1795, one guinea to subscribers.[20] The oil painting, now at Greenwich, was at some indeterminate time reduced in size all round to 259 x 366 cm / 102 x 144 in, which accounts for partly missing figures and other details which are all present on the print. A number of the portraits also appeared as separate small prints plus an informative key to the whole. Two versions of this were issued, perhaps the larger when the picture was exhibited and the other with the print, identifying both personnel and the ships shown: *Ramillies, Brunswick, La Juste, Gibraltar, Royal George, Sans Pareil* and *Glory*.[21]

From Midshipman Dillon's memoirs there is a good account of the exhibition, though writing years after the event he confuses it to some degree with a rival attraction in the Historic Gallery, Pall Mall.[22] This was of what is now the most famous picture of the action by the Alsatian-born Philippe-Jacques de Louther- bourg (1740–1812), French and British Academician, pioneering scenic director of the Drury Lane Theatre under Garrick and Sheridan, proto-cinematographer, freemason, faith-healer and mystic—and one of the great men of the international romantic movement.[23]

De Loutherbourg's 'Lord Howe's action, or the Glorious First of June' (see Fig. 7.viii), is an astonishing story of a work which started off with one companion piece and ended with another. It was painted in 1795 for £500 on commission to the publishers V.

and R. Green and Christian von Mechel, as a pair to a similarly sized and priced military work of 1793–94, 'The Siege of Valenciennes' by the Duke of York (May–July 1793); in both he had help from James Gillray on the figures. It was on show in the Historic Gallery, with the Valenciennes, entry 1 shilling, from 2 March 1795, apparently with de Loutherbourg in attendance.[24] However, James Fittler's print was only issued in January 1799 and that of Valenciennes not until 1801. Both pictures were sold in 1799 to a Mr T. Vernon of Liverpool and became well-known patriotic pieces, through the prints and further exhibition (in Edinburgh for example in 1800). They were subsequently split, the Valenciennes ending up in Lord Hesketh's collection at Easton Neston and the de Loutherbourg bought for St James's Palace by the Prince of Wales in the early 1800s. It was the need for a new pendant to it as part of the redecoration of the Palace, after the Prince became George IV, which led to the Royal commission of Turner's 'Trafalgar' of 1823—a work so controversial that the King gave both paintings to Greenwich Hospital six years later.[25] In this instance at least our debt to de Loutherbourg's is unusual since without it, or without its separation from the Valenciennes, the Trafalgar would never have been painted. De Loutherbourg's picture was and is often held up as nautically preferable to the Turner; on the literal representation of the ships it is, but it is no less a stirring fabrication of actual events and was disapproved of on that ground both by Lord Howe and James Bowen.[26]

The last two pictures under review are those exhibited and published as prints by A.C. de Poggi at his premises at 91 New Bond Street in 1795–96, apparently with the express sanction (if the blurb is to be credited) of Lord Howe. The artist in this case was Robert Cleveley 'of the Royal Navy' (1747–1809).[27] He of course is well-known; one of the twin sons of John Cleveley, also a marine painter, he had been a naval clerk before taking up full-time marine painting about 1777 and was subsequently appointed draughtsman to the Duke of Clarence and Marine Painter to the Prince Regent. He specialized in battles, especially for the printmakers.

The paintings in this case were another huge pair (228 x 343 cm / 90 x 138 in) one at least of which was completed in 1794

and the other presumably by 1795. The canvases surfaced from a
south London store in 1981 in dire condition and were sold by
Sotheby's that December; their whereabouts are currently unknown.[28] The large plates from them (51 x 77.5 cm / 20 x 30.5
in) were apparently first issued on 1 August 1795 but were
reissued in second state on 15 February 1796, bringing them
into line with their descriptive accompanying letterpress then
published.

The first shows the *Montagne* and the *Queen Charlotte* just after
the latter lost her foretop at about 10.45 a.m. according to this
source, though it was in fact a little earlier; 'the second . . .
exhibits an interesting and affecting scene [see Fig. 7.ix]. It
shows the respective conditions of the British and the enemy's
fleet after the engagement', Villaret bearing down 'in a compact
line' to cover the retreat of *le Républicain* and seven others (not
seen) '. . . and . . . bearing away for France while he had a
favourable wind . . .; leaving behind him in the undisputed
possession of the English, seven of his line of battle in the state of
complete wrecks. The view of the sinking of the *Vengeur*, an event
awfully sublime, is particularly expressed.'[29]

It also lays emphasis on the efforts to save the crew of the
Vengeur especially by boats of the *Alfred* and by the *Rattler* cutter.
These prints were very expensive, three guineas the pair or six
guineas proof, and the letterpress emphasized that 'Mr Robert
Cleveley . . . has endeavoured to represent those points of time
on which the decision and consequence of the battle chiefly
depended and which are in themselves strictly historical. See [it
adds] the annexed plan with the prints.'[30]

This battle plan, rather than the prints themselves, is perhaps
the most interesting aspect of the project—a detailed and finely
drawn foldout, including the artist's viewpoint for both pictures.
There was also a separate numbered key relating the pictures to
the plan. Overall this combination of paintings, plates, plan, key
and printed commentary is rare if not unique and can only have
been the result of extensive research. The plan and key were only
issued on 5 and 25 March 1796 respectively, so while the separate
interpretative elements do make up a whole, one is left wonder-
ing whether de Poggi in fact delayed issuing his second state of
the prints until this full apparatus was available. All the artists,

Fig. 7.ix. The end of the battle, engraved by T. Medland after the second of Robert Cleveley's large oil paintings; with the Vengeur sinking, centre left, and Villaret's remaining ships making their escape on the right. NMM PAH7876.

or their principals, of course infested Portsmouth and the fleet in the aftermath of the battle.

As is well known, the original French version of the loss of the *Vengeur* is rather different: that she sank but did not surrender. Nicholas Ozanne the Younger's plate (Fig. 7.x), undated but near contemporary, is the visual equivalent of Barère's report to the Convention to that effect and could hardly be otherwise since his fiction is appended to it as letterpress.[31] Even the ship's captain, the undeniably heroic Renaudin, disowned the 'no surrender' myth but it remained potent. Around 1870 there was a late boom in French prints rehearsing it, more perhaps than issued at the time of the action. The National Maritime Museum holds at least four colour lithographs, all of about that date or style, of which three are from numbered series. An oil in the same vein, dated 1873, by Hendrick Schaefels (1827–1904) was also recently sold in London.[32] A possible explanation for this phenomenon is that it may have been less to do with 'le Combat du Treize Prairial', to use the French name for the action, and more related to a general effusion of historical patriotism triggered by foundation of the Third Republic in 1871, after the Franco-Prussian War.

However, by far the largest contemporary view of the battle was that exhibited at the Panorama, in Cranbourne Street, Leicester Square. The building, specifically designed to accommodate the entirely circular views patented by Robert Barker (1739–1806) as 'la nature à coup d'oeil' in 1787—the name 'panorama' was later supplied by a friend—had itself only been opened in May 1793.[33] Visitors who stood on the central viewing platform were persuaded by the concealed illumination (a masked overhead skylight) and the absence of other reference points, that they really stood in the scene portrayed—usually a city-scape, or in the midst of a battle by land or sea. The picture was on 10,000 square feet of canvas comprising a drum 27.7m / 90ft across (about 87m / 283ft unrolled) and 10.75m / 35ft high. The opening view, by Barker, had been that of the Grand Fleet at Spithead during the Russian armament of 1791 and in the spring of 1795 this was replaced by his rendering of the close of the Battle of First of June. It opened apparently on the action's first anniversary, about 2 June 1795 being the closest known date, and

Fig. 7.x. Combat du Vengeur: Yves le Gouaz's print after the painting by Nicholas Ozanne the Younger. *NMM PAD5451.*

drew crowds to April 1796, when a successor showing Alexander Hood, Lord Bridport's Action off Groix, replaced it:[34]

> Captain Barlow of the Pegasus, Lord Howe's repeating frigate, and Captain Seymour [then lieutenant], who was signal officer with Captain Barlow at that time, having obligingly furnished . . . a correct plan of the situation of every ship, taken the first moment they could be discovered from the smoke . . . Observers may suppose themselves on the open Sea in the centre of both fleets . . . near the Queen Charlotte . . .[35]

An American visitor marvelled: 'nothing can be seen but sky and water, and the beholder thinks himself on the Ocean surrounded by ships of war in action. The whole has a fine effect and exceeds any idea I had formed of painting. Admittance 1 shilling.'[36] It was the first of many naval battle panoramas subsequently painted by Barker and others. Nelson himself thanked Barker for perpetuating the fame of the Battle of the Nile in this way when they met at Palermo in 1799, news of its success at Cranbourne Street having reached him there.[37]

Of more directly theatrical spin-offs there are three currently known. At Sadlers Wells, in 1794, the house scenic artist Robert Andrews produced a scene or scenes for a piece called 'Naval Triumph, the metropolis during rejoicings and illuminations'—apparently though not certainly a reflection on the battle—following it in 1795 by one called 'England's Glory', based on de Loutherbourg's picture.[38] This can only have been from a surreptitious sketch of it as exhibited, or possibly from a pirated print of similar origin. Such a print certainly existed, but whether before or after the 1799 official version is unknown.[39]

By far the most important theatrical event, however, was that put on at the Theatre Royal Drury Lane by its manager-playwright Richard Brinsley Sheridan on Wednesday 2 July 1794 as an afterpiece to *The Country Girl*. Got up from start to finish in three days, including painting the scenery, writing the script and full rehearsal, this was a brief interlude entitled *The Glorious First of June*. It took place under the patronage of a very elevated committee, two of whom (the Duke of Leeds and the Earl of Mulgrave) supplied songs which were incorporated in dialogue put together by Sheridan and James Cobb, with a prologue by the novelist Joseph Richardson; the verse quoted at the beginning of this paper is from Mulgrave's contribution. The very slight plot is immaterial but involves 'jack tars', their pining sweethearts, an old commodore and a comic lawyer (Dicky Suett reviving and extending his popular role of Endless from *No Song, No Supper*, a well-known farce in the Theatre's repertory). There is also a spectacular concluding sea-fight pageant with model ships and explosions, very reminiscent of de Loutherbourg's 1779 staging of the Spanish Armada in Sheridan's *The Critic*. This ended with a portrait transparency and firework tableau honouring Lord Howe. The much applauded nautical scenes are well described in newspaper accounts, all reprinted in the standard modern edition of Sheridan.[40] I know of no illustration but the scenery was probably by Thomas Greenwood, who in 1779 produced a naval transparency for Sadler's Wells, showing the young Duke of Clarence flanked by Admirals Digby and Rodney, of which an engraving survives to indicate how such things looked.[41]

There are two important points about Sheridan's piece. It was again a first of its sort, got up quite expressly to raise funds for the relief of the widows and orphans of Lord Howe's action. Sheridan himself was a personal friend of the rakish Captain John Payne of the 74-gun *Russell*, fourth in Howe's line, and wrote to him about his intentions in this regard. Everyone involved, including a good cast, provided their services free for the benefit night, which took £1,526.11s—the largest sum gained by any single theatre performance at either Drury Lane or Covent Garden during the eighteenth century.[42] It was subsequently repeated only six times in 1794, to very average results of about £220–320 in nightly takings, but was revived in altered form in 1797 to mark the Battle of Cape St Vincent.[43]

Finally of course, appropriately, and just a month from the event it celebrated, Sheridan's interlude fulfilled the Shakespearean role of the stage in 'holding the mirror up to nature'. For if its content was quickly forgotten its title was to become that by which Howe's action remains best known. The epithet 'glorious' had been much in the air, as it was for many victories, but its first adoption in a nascently titular form seems to have been an advertisement Sheridan put in *The Times* of 13 June

1794, the day the fleet returned, announcing an impromptu celebration at the Theatre that evening.[44] It presumably struck the right chord, if only in Sheridan's mind, to become the title of his slightly more considered piece. To borrow a line from his most famous creation, Mrs Malaprop in *The Rivals*, it showed his gift for 'a nice derangement of epitaphs', which two centuries of general use have now endorsed.

Notes

I would like to acknowledge the assistance of Derek Forbes, my colleague in the Society for Theatre Research, in preparing this paper; also that of Ralph Hyde and the advice of Professor Paul Webb. The paintings with a BHC reference number appear in *The Concise Catalogue of Oil Paintings in the National Maritime Museum* (Woodbridge, 1988). Sizes of prints were noted to indicate general scale only when this paper was delivered and are of the image, letterpress excluded, to the nearest ¼ in (5mm). Readers may also be interested in Stephen Conway's more recently written article which, using documentary sources, covers related ground for the Battle of the Saints, 1782: 'A Joy Unknown for Years Past: The American War, Britishness and the Celebration of Rodney's Victory at the Saints' in *History* 282 (2001) pp. 180–99.

1. Ben's song, by Lord Mulgrave, from 'The Glorious First of June' in Cecil Price (ed.), *The Dramatic Works of Richard Brinsley Sheridan*, (Oxford, 1973) Vol. II, pp. 772–73.
2. In 1828, H.P. Briggs retrospectively painted George III's visit to the fleet and his presentation of a jewelled sword to Lord Howe. Exhibited at the British Institution (BI) that year, the BI immediately presented it to Greenwich Hospital and it is now in the National Maritime Museum (NMM BHC0476) as are some of the medals awarded including Alexander Hood's flag-officer's medal, with its gold chain, and Collingwood's as flag-captain of the *Culloden* to Rear Admiral Sir George Bowyer. See p. 166 below.
3. Harry Parker, *Naval Battles, from the collection of prints formed and owned by Commander Sir Charles Lionel Cust . . .* (London, 1911). The NMM copy (Pictures Section) is in two interleaved volumes with substantial Ms additions to the printed listings. All relate to historical representations, not caricature commemoratives.

4. See David Cordingly, *Nicholas Pocock* (London, 1986).

5. Serres was from the fringes of aristocracy and was nephew of an archbishop, as well as being Marine Painter to George III; see E.H.H. Archibald, *Dictionary of Sea Painters* (2nd edn, Woodbridge, 1989).

6. See Cordingly, pp. 69–72 and 109–16 for discussion, illustrations and full transcription of Pocock's notes. I have not clarified the relation between the *Brunswick* account by Lieutenant Rowland Bevan which Pocock preserved and that by him published by W.G. Perrin in 1928 (*Naval Miscellany*, NRS vol. LXIII, pp. 155–169). Pocock's notebook is now in the NMM (MS JOD 12) as are the separate sketches mentioned.

7. His view of the *Brunswick* engaging *L'Achille* and *Vengeur*, dated 1796 and exhibited that year at the Royal Academy, was purchased by Sir James Caird for the NMM in 1934 (BHC0471). He showed two of Rear Admiral Sir Thomas Pasley and the *Bellerophon*'s involvment in 1798 and 1801, while his small 1811 view of the *Defence* in action, was apparently for her captain (later admiral) James Gambier, whose family presented it to Greenwich Hospital in 1865 (NMM BHC0474); Cordingly, pls 52–53, illustrates both the NMM pictures.

8. The large aquatint plates were both the *Brunswick* and *Vengeur*, one (48 x 65cm, eng. R. Pollard) dated 16 February 1796, being a version of the exhibited oil composition (NMM PAH7865), the other (42 x 60.5cm, eng. R. Pollard and J. Whidnell) showing the *Brunswick* broadside on and the *Vengeur* sinking (NMM PAH7866). The *Naval Chronicle* aquatint plates appeared as follows: vol. I (1799) pls i, iv, v, xx; vol. II (1800) pl. xxxi.

9. NMM PAD5467, eng. Walker, pub B. Crosby. One of the ships appears to be flying Dutch colours which suggests it might relate to the Dogger Bank action of 1781, though I have not located such an example.

10. A copy of the *Morning Herald* plan is included in Pocock's battle notebook and in the NMM copy of *Official Documents . . . of the Glorious Victory . . . on Sunday June 1 1794* (Debrett, London 1794).

11. One shows the close of action (NMM PAH7872), engraved by R. Pollard and J. Wells, and published by R. Pollard, Spa Fields; the other shows the fleet bringing the prizes into Spithead (PAH 7880), engraved by Pollard and Birnie and published by John Jeffrys, Ludgate Hill.

12. NMM PAH7861.

13. NMM PAH7862, the fleet regaining the wind of the enemy on 29 May; PAH7863, breaking the line on 1 June. Both engraved by Evans (40 x 60cm).

14. NMM BHC0469. Sir James Caird bought it for the NMM via the Parker Gallery in 1933 for £1,000, in circumstances well recorded in the NMM picture file. Dodd had lived nearby in Lucas Place. In January 1831, the marine artist George Chambers painted a stage panorama of the 'Glorious First' for the nearby Pavilion Theatre and would certainly have known the Dodd canvas, though no direct connection is provable.

15. NMM PAH7864 and 7873, both by Henry Whitmarsh Pearse and published by T. Whitewood, Portsea, 1 July 1796.

16. Copley's involvment is covered in Richard D. Altick, *The Shows of London* (Cambridge, MA, 1979), pp. 105–6.

17. This is owned by the City of London, Guildhall Collection. It has now (2001) been magnificently restored and is the centrepiece of the new Guildhall Art Gallery.

18. BHC2790, Caird purchase, 1933.

19. See Dorinda Evans, *Mather Brown, Early American Artist in England*, (Middletown, CT, 1982) pp. 127–30, and 247. 'Captain' Neville was in fact only a lieutenant.

20. NMM PAH7878 (proof before title) and 7879; (43 x 48cm / 17 x 22¾in).

21. NMM holds copies of the keys and one also appeared in the *Britannic Magazine*, 1795; see Evans, p. 189 n.12. The canvas ended up at Hartwell Hall, Chorley, in about 1850. This later became a hotel and was pulled down in 1937–38 when Sir James Caird bought the picture for NMM for £500 (BHC2740).

22. Michael Lewis (ed.), Sir William Henry Dillon, *A Narrative of my Professional Adventures (1790–1839)*, vol. I, (Navy Records Society, 1953), pp. 157–58.

23. For de Loutherbourg see Christopher Baugh, *Garrick and Loutherbourg* (London, 1990) and R. Joppien, *Philippe Jacques de Loutherbourg R.A. 1740–1812* (GLC, Kenwood House, exh. cat. 1973).

24. Joppien, ibid., nos 64 and 65; Dillon, loc. cit.; Altick, p. 136.

25. The controversy is briefly covered in Martin Butlin and Evelyn Joll, *The Paintings of J.M.W. Turner* (London, 1977) vol. I, no. 252, pp. 139–40. De Loutherbourg's canvas measures 266.5 x 373.5 cm / 105 x 147 ins (NMM BHC0470). The Turner is 257.5 x 362.5 cm / 103 x 145in.

26. Dillon, p. 158n.; cf. Evans, *Mather Brown*, p. 189 n.17. Bowen took exception to both paintings and Howe considered de Loutherbourg's version 'as a libel on his flagship the Queen Charlotte'; W.T. Whitley, *Artists and their friends in England, 1700–99* (London, 1928) vol. II, p. 64, citing James, *Naval History* (1826). The prime objection appears to have been that had the *Queen Charlotte* managed to get alongside the *Montagne*, as de Loutherbourg shows it, the latter would not have escaped; loss of her foretopmast prevented this.

27. Cleveley was so described on the resultant prints and in de Poggi's accompanying letterpress. This consists of two parts: (1) *A Narrative of the Proceedings of H.M. Fleet under the Command of Earl Howe from the second of May to the second of June 1794* which is 100 pages, dated 1796 and does not refer directly to the pictures: (2) a separately printed descriptive 'advertisement', *Two Prints from Pictures painted by Mr Robert Cleveley* . . . , dated February 1796. This is paginated as an 11-page continuation of the *Narrative* for binding purposes, though the page numbering is confused. The foldout plan and key referred to are bound into the NMM copy used here (unique item no. E3545), the latter only in photostat form.

28. Sotheby's, *British Paintings*, 9 Dec. 1981, lots 142–3: the pair was split and fetched £15,000 and £17,000 each. The chronologically earlier scene (lot 142), showing the *Queen Charlotte* closing on the *Montagne*, is signed and dated 1794, but appears to have lost 43cm of its original width. This one was engraved by B.T. Pouncy (NMM unnumbered copy), the other by T. Medland (NMM PAH 7876).

29. *A Narrative* . . . p. 102 [recte 110].

30. ibid., p. 98 [recte 106].

31. NMM PAD 5451, eng., Y. le Gouaz.

32. Christie's South Kensington, 5 May 1994, lot 113. Of the different series to which the *c.*1870 prints belong, that by A. Mayer is no. 13 of 'Episodes Maritimes', one by Ferdinand Perrot 'no. 39' and one by Charles Leduc 'no. 49' without further identification (NMM PAH7868–70).

33. For a summary history of the Panorama, see Altick, Ch. 10.

34. A chronology of the Barker panoramas is given in Scott Barnes Wilcox, *The Panorama and related exhibitions in London* (M. Litt thesis, Edinburgh Univ., 1976) Appendix C.

35. Unidentified press cutting, John Johnson Collection, Bodleian

Library (panoramas box); the *Pegasus* link raises a possible Pocock connection. Barker's panoramas also had characteristic circular printed keys to help identify incident: many copies survive and the NMM has one for this and other panoramas.

36. Journal of John Aspinwall (1774–1847), American merchant; NMM (CIRI card file) extract supplied by Mrs Aileen Collins, 1978.
37. Altick, p. 136.
38. Sybil Rosenfeld and Edward Croft-Murray, 'Checklist of [18th-century] Scene-Painters' in *Theatre Notebook* XIX, (1964), p. 8 and XX, (1965/6), p. 69.
39. NMM PAH7874, eng., Fr. Weber and published by him and S. Tessari, London; n.d.
40. See Price n.1 above; full discussion and the text of the piece, not published at the time, is on pp. 753–74.
41. Sybil Rosenfeld, 'A Transparency by Thomas Greenwood the Elder' in *Theatre Notebook* XIX, (1964), pp. 21–22 and pl. 2.
42. Charles Beecher Hogan (ed.) *The London Stage, Part Five 1776–1800* (Carbondale, 1968), vol. III, pp. 1570, 1663–64.
43. According to *The London Stage* listing the last performance in 1794 was on 18 October; the Cape St Vincent revival saw ten performances, 6 March–17 April 1797.
44. The use of 'the glorious 1st of June' (*sic*) in *The Times* of 13 June was pointed out to me by Hugh Owen; see his subsequent note in *Mariner's Mirror* LXXX (1994), p. 336. The advertisement probably also appeared in other papers.

8

The Battle Sanctified
Some Memorials and Relics

Barbara Tomlinson

People try to preserve the memory of transient events, such as naval battles, through the preservation or creation of three-dimensional objects. For the Battle of the Glorious First of June, a large number of such objects have been preserved in museums, in private hands and in public places. They can be divided into three basic types: relics, commercial or private commemoratives and state commemorations and awards.

The term 'relics' applies to items which have been preserved because of their physical association with the battle. The most important in the collections of the National Maritime Museum are three flags which also have a symbolic significance. In the past, historic flags were treated a little like those semi-sacred ethnographic objects which, in some cultures, are deliberately exposed until they decay. It has always been difficult to reconcile display with preservation. Even today, the idea of flags as items of academic interest in themselves, rather than as sacred survivors of some important event, has only partially been accepted. The three Glorious First of June flags owe their preservation to the fact that they remained in family hands rather than being laid up in a church. Since being transferred to the museum's collections, the size, physical fragility and demanding conservation requirements of the two larger flags mean that they have had to remain in store rather than on display.

The first of these flags may be the only complete pre-1801 white ensign in existence. It was preserved because it was believed to have been worn by Captain John Harvey's ship *Brunswick* during her famous duel with *Vengeur*. It would have been seen as a patriotic symbol. Recalling Harvey's last words, the *Naval Chronicle* describes him being led below, mortally wounded 'casting a languid, yet affectionate look towards his brave crew—Persevere, my brave lads, in your duty! Continue the Action with spirit for the honour of our King and Country; and remember my last words—THE COLOURS OF THE BRUNSWICK SHALL NEVER BE STRUCK!'.[1]

The Harvey family preserved it as a memento to an illustrious ancestor. It was lent to the Royal Naval Exhibition of 1891 by Captain F. Harvey RN, and presented to the museum by Lieutenant Colonel S.F. Harvey Williams in 1953.[2] The construction is quite different from a modern white ensign. It is hand sewn and made of loosely hand-woven wool bunting. The Union Flag in the canton is without St Patrick's saltire, and the whole design is very inaccurately made up. The size is 6.25 x 12.07 m. All this is quite consistent with a 1794 date.

The legend, however is probably incorrect. It was decided before the battle that to avoid confusion with the French colours, red ensigns should be worn by all British ships in place of white squadronal colours. Some ships had their ensigns shot away, and hoisted white ones in their place, but the *Brunswick* is shown in a painting after Pocock, still wearing her red ensign at the close of the action.[3] Our ensign may be her squadronal colours or have belonged to some other member of the Harvey family, which included five naval officers at the time. This sort of inconsistency in the provenance of historic flags is not uncommon.

The museum also has on loan the Union Flag flown at the main of *Queen Charlotte* by Howe as acting Admiral of the Fleet (see Fig. 8.i), which can be seen in the de Loutherbourg painting of the action. It was preserved by Lieutenant William Burgh who was present during the action and lent to the museum by a descendant. The construction is similar to the white ensign and the size is 3.96 x 5.59 m.

Fig. 8.i. 'Lord Howe, Union at the main': The pre-1801 Union flag flown at the main truck of the Queen Charlotte *by Howe as commander-in-chief, 1 June 1794. It measures approximately 4 x 6 m. NMM AAA0730.*

The third flag is the banner of the boarding division of the French ship *L'America* captured by the *Leviathan* commanded by Lord Hugh Seymour (see Fig. 8.ii). As a military flag, it is a much more manageable size, 686 x 660 mm. It is made of white linen embroidered with the battle cry 'MARINS LA REPUBLIQUE OU LA MORT'. Perhaps the banner provides some evidence of an attempt to carry out the ideas of Jeanbon Saint André: 'Disdaining skilful evolution . . . perhaps our seamen will think it more fitting and useful to try those boarding actions in which the Frenchman was always a conqueror'.[4] No doubt many such banners were produced in readiness for action. This one is a rare survival.

Storing a flag is a relatively inexpensive form of commemoration. The state was much more lavish in its attempts to reward its naval heroes and promote patriotic fervour. The

Fig. 8.ii. 'Sailors, the Republic or Death': Banner of the boarding division of the French 74, L' America, which was engaged and captured by the British Leviathan on 1 June 1794. NMM AAA0564.

striking difference between public memorials erected at the end of the eighteenth century and those put up by public subscription from the mid-nineteenth century, is the earlier lack of monuments to collective casualties of war, shipwrecks or other disasters. The eighteenth century commemorated individual heroes at considerable public expense. As far as the navy was concerned, heroes were of the rank of captain and above.

The first monument to a naval hero to be voted by Parliament was that to Captain James Cornwall, killed on 1 February 1744, in the controversial action off Toulon. The battle was followed by a House of Commons enquiry and the courts martial of several of the officers involved. The memorial was more a reproof to the government of the day by an opposition faction playing the patriotic card, than the celebration of a national triumph. In contrast to the indecisive actions of this earlier period, the latter part of the eighteenth century saw a great improvement in British naval fortunes. A Treasury committee was set up in 1796 to commission a series of monuments to contemporary heroes, both naval and military. A second one was formed in 1802.[5]

As the Revolutionary Wars continued, the Glorious First of June was seen as the first of a series of victories. The Westminster Abbey memorial to Captain John Harvey and Captain John Hutt of the *Queen* by John Bacon the Younger was not completed until 1804. Both lost a limb in action, both died on the same day and the *Naval Chronicle* made much of the fact that they both shared a post-chaise from London whilst travelling to join their ships. The lower part of the monument showed a relief of a naval engagement (as the two officers were engaged in different parts of the action, this was left a little vague), with a flying angel representing Providence holding a palm branch for victory and a pair of scales representing the justice of the British cause. At some time before 1812, this lower section was moved to the church of St Mary the Virgin at Eastry, Kent, where John Harvey's remains were buried.[6] The inscription on the pyramid subsequently placed above the relief commemorates John Harvey and other members of his family, but not John Hutt. The upper part of the memorial with its figures of fame and Britannia on either side of an urn bearing portraits of the two officers, remains in the Abbey.

The other Glorious First of June monument in the Abbey was commissioned directly by the Treasury for 3,500 guineas in 1798. It commemorates Captain James Montagu who was also killed in the action and is by the eminent sculptor John Flaxman (see Fig. 8.iii). A full length statue of Montagu in contemporary uniform stands on top of a cylindrical base with a relief of the battle on the front. The image corresponds to an aquatint after

*Fig. 8.iii. Monument to Captain James Montagu in Westminster Abbey,
by John Flaxman.*

Robert Dodd with Howe's flagship the *Queen Charlotte* in the centre of the picture.[7]

Flaxman also produced a more elaborate memorial to Lord Howe, who died in 1799. It was commissioned for 6,000 guineas in 1803 and erected in St Pauls. The uniformed figure of Howe is attended by female figures representing Fame and Victory while the British lion lies at his feet. Britannia is seated at the back on a classicized version of the hull of the *Queen Charlotte*. In Flaxman's original drawing, the admiral in classical dress is being crowned by the winged figure of the goddess Victory. This earlier design is much closer to prototypes drawn from the ancient world than the completed version.

In contrast to these expensive public monuments are the modest family memorials to officers of lower rank, or to those who survived the action. Admiral Sir Roger Curtis (d. 1816) has a wall tablet among the other Curtis memorials at St James's Church, Clanfield, Hampshire. Captain Andrew Snape Douglas and Lieutenant Francis Ross have table tombs at Fulham, London, and Topsham, Devon, respectively. The former died in June 1797, possibly as a result of a head injury sustained during the battle. The latter, killed in the action, has a charmingly naive epitaph composed by his son:

> One vengeful ball by battle sped,
> A gallant spirit flies;
> Blue surges close above his head,
> In ocean's depths he lies.
> A severed trunk—no warning given,
> One moment warm with life;
> Buoyant with hope, and trust in heaven,
> The next past mortal strife.
>
> Yield up—yield up—thou mighty sea,
> Restore thy prey to light;
> Death has been vanquished, souls are free,
> Stand forth, redeem'd in might.

Other official awards were presented directly by the crown. When George III visited Lord Howe on board the *Queen Charlotte* on 26 June, he presented him with a diamond-hilted and enamelled sword, an event shown in a painting by Henry Briggs.[8] In common with other presentation swords of the time, it is more an item of jewellery than a functional weapon, and bears an inscription, relating the circumstances of its presentation. The sword is still in existence in the possession of the family.

On the same occasion, the king presented the admirals who had participated in the action with gold chains.[9] Two years later, he sent them gold medals to be worn on the chains. A portrait of Admiral Curtis wearing the chain without the medal is in the possession of the Curtis family. A smaller gold medal was sent to fourteen of the twenty-five post-captains who commanded ships of the line in the battle. The neo-classical design on the obverse shows Britannia standing on an ancient galley holding a spear, her right foot on a helmet, the union shield behind her. She is being crowned with a wreath by a small figure of Victory, winged and holding a palm branch. The captain's medal was suspended by a blue and white ribbon as were the Naval Gold Medals issued for subsequent actions. They were eventually superseded by the Military Order of the Bath which was refounded in 1815.

A more populist attitude towards military commemoration and awards became apparent in the mid-nineteenth century, when Queen Victoria instituted the Naval General Service Medal. She wished to introduce a naval medal for those of lower rank present at naval actions for which the Naval Gold Medal had been awarded. An enthusiastic committee extended this to include 231 naval engagements in all. Those veterans of the Glorious First who survived until 1849 were duly awarded their Naval General Service Medals suspended on a blue and white ribbon, a deliberate imitation of the ribbon of the Naval Gold Medal.

In addition to these public and private memorials and medals, many commercial commemoratives were produced. There is evidence that ceramic manufacturers initially adapted some lines already in production, relating perhaps to the previous war. Sotheby's, Chester, in their sale of 8 October 1986, lot 501, included a typical Rodney mask jug with an inscription on the base indicating that it now commemorated Lord Howe. An earthenware jug in the National Maritime Museum's collection bears an oval medallion of a ship at sea with 'Ad Howe' below. It is an example of the sort of general maritime design easily adapted to a topical battle or personality. A mezzotint published by Laurie and Whittle on 11 June 1794 is inscribed 'Right Honble. Richard Lord Howe Commander in Chief of His Majesty's Fleet in the Channel'. Howe's appointment to this command took place in 1793, so the print had been somewhat overtaken by events. It was nevertheless used to decorate a Leeds creamware mug, an example of which is now in the collections of the National Maritime Museum.

As the war continued and the Glorious First was seen as one of many triumphs, higher quality depictions of Howe were produced as one of a group of successful admirals. The Derby factory produced figures of Howe, Rodney and Hood in biscuit porcelain. The modeller is thought to have been Pierre Stephan (fl. 1770–95).[10] The British Museum has an example of the figure of Howe. A different version in glazed porcelain is in the Willett Collection at Brighton Museum. Wedgwood medallions of Howe, Duncan, Nelson and St Vincent were produced in 1798 modelled by John de Vaere. These four portraits have been used to decorate a stoneware mug by William Adams & Sons of Tunstall. In the same year, James Tassie produced a similar but more informal portrait medallion in glass paste.

The tradition of striking commemorative medals to celebrate military victories started during the early Renaissance and continued through intervening centuries up to the period under discussion. Although the designs harked back to Roman coins, they were not always produced at the initiative of governments, being sometimes struck by individuals. The early nineteenth century saw a flowering of the art of the medallist in Britain. A commemorative medal by C.H. Kuchler shows a profile bust of Howe on the obverse and *Queen Charlotte* sinking an opponent on the reverse.[11] The Glorious First of June is also commemorated as one of a series of National Medals issued by James Mudie between 1814–20. This production was inspired by Vivant Denon's scheme in France, which aimed to commemorate the victories of Napoleon in the manner that the 'Medallic Histories' of the seventeenth century had commemorated those of Louis XIV. On Mudie's medal, a bust of the admiral once again features on the obverse and Neptune in a chariot drawn by sea horses on the reverse. The medallist was the famous William Wyon.[12]

A more elaborate form of the same iconography features on a pewter medal in the National Maritime Museum's collections. The obverse shows Howe once again while the reverse shows Neptune pointing to the battle with one hand and handing a trident to Britannia with the other. Beside her, cornucopias spill coins. Behind them, winged Victory hovers over an obelisk on which are inscribed the names of the flag officers who took part in the battle.

This allusive neo-classical imagery, with allegorical figures representing victory, fame, commercial prosperity, patriotism and domination of the sea, unites many of the disparate forms by which naval battles were commemorated at the end of the eighteenth century. This language, also present in France, suggests a uniform cultural movement affecting both countries, and reveals an affinity which contrasts with the conflicting ideologies that divided them.

Notes

1. *Naval Chronicle*, vol. III, p. 257.
2. *Official Catalogue, Royal Naval Exhibition 1891*, exhibit 2980.
3. NMM Collections, BHC0473.
4. Oliver Warner, *The Glorious First of June* (London, 1961), p. 62.
5. David Irwin, *John Flaxman, Sculptor, Illustrator, Designer* (Studio Vista/Christies, 1961), pp. 156–62.
6. Information from Westminster Abbey Library.
7. NMM Collections.
8. Ibid. BHC0476.
9. Kenneth Douglas Morris, *Naval Medals 1793–1956* (London, 1987), pp. 10–12, 20–21.
10. Surgeon Captain P.D. Gordon Pugh, *Naval Ceramics* (Newport, 1971), p. 21.
11. Admiral the Marquess of Milford Haven, *British Naval Medals* (London, 1919), pp. 210–126.
12. Mark Jones, *The Art of the Medal* (British Museum, 1979), p. 105.

Contributors

Dr André Delaporte studied at the Sorbonne and Lycée Condorcet in Paris, at universities in Rennes and Nantes, and has lectured in history at Bastia, Corsica, Trier in Germany, and in Paris. In 1993–94, he was Chief of the Historical Section of the Service historique de la Marine in Vincennes, after which he returned to teaching at Rochefort. He has published numerous papers in both French and foreign journals.

Chris Ware has recently retired from the National Maritime Museum whose Historical Section he entered in 1977. He has published papers on the Royal Navy and the Plantations *c* 1720–30 and on the Royal Navy at Toulon in 1793. His book *The Bomb Vessel* was published by Conway Maritime Press in 1994.

Dr Roger Morris was a Curator at the National Maritime Museum until 1995. He is now a lecturer in the University of Exeter Centre for Maritime Historical Studies. His books include *The Royal Dockyards during the Revolutionary and Napoleonic Wars* (Leicester, 1983), *Guide to British naval papers in North America* (London, 1994), *Cockburn and the British Navy in Transition. Admiral Sir George Cockburn 1772–1853* (Exeter, 1997), and *The Chnnel Fleet and the Blockade of Brest 1793–1801* (Navy Records Society, 2001).

Dr Michael Duffy is Head of History and Director of the Centre for Maritime Historical Studies at the University of Exeter. His books include *The Military Revolution and the State* (Exeter, 1983), *The Englishman and the Foreigner* (Cambridge, 1986), *Soldiers, Sugar and Seapower. The British expeditions to the Caribbean and the War against Revolutionary France* (Oxford, 1987), *Parameters of British Naval Power, 1650–1850* (Exeter, 1992), *The New Maritime History of Devon* (London, 1992, 1994) and *The Younger Pitt* (London, 2000). From 1990 to 2000 he was the editor of *The Mariner's Mirror, The Journal of the Society for Nautical Research.*

Professor Lawrence Evans was brought up in Manchester, England, but went to the USA during the Second World War as a Communications Officer on loan from the Royal Navy to the Norwegian Merchant navy. He was educated at and taught in a number of American universities before joining the State University of New York at Binghamton in 1967. He specialized in international relations and United States foreign policy, writing also on economics and maritime affairs. Sadly Professor Evans died just before the conference to mark the anniversary of the Battle of the Glorious First of June in 1994, where his paper was read for him by Dr Roger Knight.

Dr Pieter van der Merwe holds degrees in drama from the Universities of Manchester, where he also worked in stage design, and Bristol. He joined the National Maritime Museum in 1974, where the first of his many display projects was to assist development of new eighteenth-century galleries, including that covering the Glorious First of June. He is currently the Museum's General Editor and has published in the fields of maritime art and archaeology, and in the history of theatre and public exhibitions.

Barbara Tomlinson worked for five years at the Science Museum, London, before joining the National Maritime Museum in 1978. She worked in the Pictures Department before transferring to the Department of Weapons and Antiquities. She is now in the Research Department. Her special interests and publications are in flags, maritime related church monuments and polar exploration.

Index

Printed and bound by CPI Group (UK) Ltd, Croydon, CR0 4YY

13/04/2025

14656587-0005